FISHING THE OREGON COUNTRY

Revised Edition

By Francis H. Ames

Pencil Illustrations by George M. Davis

Introduction by Ted Trueblood

Preface to the Revised Edition by Dan Casali

Flying Pencil Publications
Portland, Oregon
1988

Revised Edition ©1988 by Flying Pencil Publications.
All rights reserved
including the right of reproduction
in whole or in part in any form

First Edition © 1966 by The Caxton Printers, Ltd.
First printing May, 1966
Second printing May, 1969
Third printing April 1972

Pencil illustrations © 1988 by George M. Davis, artist

Published by Flying Pencil Publications
P.O. Box 19062
Portland, Oregon 97219
Manufactured in the United States of America

10 9 8 7 6 5 4 3 2 1

Library of Congress Cataloging in Publication Data

Ames, Francis H.
  Fishing the Oregon country.
  1. Fishing--Oregon. I. Title.
SH539.A6 1988   799.109795   87-83635

ISBN 0-916473-02-3

CONTENTS

Francis H. Ames
1900-1986

Raised on a hardscrabble ranch on the dry plains of eastern Montana, Francis Ames (Frank to his friends) had two overwhelming ambitions in life—to be a writer and a fisherman.

The nearest school was a cold five-mile hike from the family ranch, and the nearest place where a boy could wet his fishing line was a muddy water tank fifty miles away. Yet when Frank Ames died in July, 1986, he had realized both of his dreams.

He first started fishing Oregon waters in 1926. By the time he sat down to write this book, he was a forty year veteran of Oregon country angling and a regular columnist for national outdoor publications, with nearly six-hundred published fishing and hunting magazine articles and short stories to his credit, as well as three novels based on his Montana boyhood.

Frank Ames settled permanently in Oregon in the 1930s, living with his wife Laura in a cabin near Rose Lodge, above the Salmon River. And while he favored the Salmon, and perhaps the North Fork Yamhill a little above all others, it could be said that the Oregon Country itself was his *home stream*. With migratorial instincts honed by years of observation, investigation, and practice, Frank Ames travelled the state tuned to the seasons, in pursuit of fish and fishing know-how.

George M. Davis, Artist
1926 -

George M. Davis brings to Frank Ames' work the invaluable contribution of the skilled artist who is himself a life-long fisher of the Oregon country. A fifth generation Oregonian, whose ancestors homesteaded Eastern Oregon, George Davis is a professional water-colorist specializing in landscapes and wildlife of the Pacific Northwest.

FOREWORD TO THE REVISED EDITION

My Oregon fishing experience began while I was a graduate student at the University of Oregon in Eugene. I had only taken up the challenge of trout and fly the year before, in the high desert of northern New Mexico. I was green as green could be, and I soon learned that an *exceptional* rating on a water was no guarantee that *I'd* have exceptional luck.

I'd drive down the McKenzie River road and gawk at local anglers dragging fish as long as your leg out to their cars (yeah, with little tail marks in the dust behind them)—but I sure couldn't catch them myself.

My graduate research time was about equally divided between the university library and the Caddis Fly flyshop. There I would try to wheedle Bob Guard out of the latest hot tips, which he used to chum up gear sales.

In those days, a second hand bookstore was located next door to the shop, and I'd often take a turn through its fishing section to scan whatever the tide had brought in. And there I first encountered and bought a well thumbed copy of *Fishing the Oregon Country*, printed nine years before. After devouring the book in a marathon read, I learned once and for all that successful fishing wasn't just a matter of luck.

That battered copy set me off on many adventures, for the hints Ames drops are irresistible to any fishing fanatic. Each time I crack the book my list of places to go and tricks to try gets longer. *Be warned:* this book will put miles on your odometer and holes in your waders. You will find yourself mumbling excuses to employer and spouse in response to certain climatological stimuli.

Twenty-two years have passed since Ames wrote, and time has brought changes to some of the waters he fished. Many changes have been for the good. Stricter environmental laws have had a positive impact on the Willamette Valley streams. Salmon and steelhead stocking programs have established runs on formerly depleted streams, enabling anglers to catch steelhead or salmon in every season.

In some cases, such as the Yamhill River, establishment of steelhead runs has meant diminished forage and habitat for the native cutthroat trout. But the Department of Fish and Wildlife has dramatically decreased the number of hatchery rainbow dumped into the broth, so the native trout has a sporting chance. The annual congregation of suckers on the Yamhill has disappeared with the permanent elimination of the dam at Carlton. Or maybe they've just moved—another tip for readers to explore. The Yamhill itself is still as pretty in spring as ever.

Browns are still plentiful in the Little Deschutes. Much land adjacent to the lower river has been developed, but the upper river around Crescent Creek is still undeveloped, and Crescent Creek itself (which is totally within national forest) has a thriving brown trout population.

The headwaters of the Big Deschutes are still a joy to fish in late spring. The river above Crane Prairie is closed till June 1 to protect spawning rainbows, and the stream has recently been cleared of obstructions all the way to Lava Lake so that the big fish migrate freely.

Ames' beloved Salmon River still puts out the fish, in fact now more than ever. There's a salmon hatchery on the river above Otis, and hatchery-reared chinook tend to dominate the fishery. The classic holes are alot more crowded with both fish and anglers, but the jacks still jump at Rose Lodge, and the upstream fishery is little changed. Sea-run cutts and silvers are there for those who follow Ames' advice.

There are more *Private Property* signs now, though the Department of Fish and Wildlife has purchased and developed additional public access points for many favorite waters. You might find streamside landowners a little less willing to allow anglers to cross their property due to the bad manners of a few, but many will permit angler access if courteously asked. Increased angler pressure makes common courtesy toward landowners all the more important. Ask permission. Leave gates as you find them. Don't leave a mess behind. Respect for the land and its owners is the most potent weapon we anglers have to retain river access. But you already know that.

Certainly there are more anglers on the waters, particularly at the traditional hot spots. But if you follow Ames' lead, you'll never lack for casting room or for streamside solitude, when that is your preference. In this volume Francis Ames both welcomes us to join in the fun of Oregon angling comraderie, and challenges us to take rod and map in hand and make our own angling discoveries.

As for fishing tackle and technique, fashions have come and gone and come again since this book was first published. But through it all, no one bothered to tell the fish!

It's a real pleasure to be able to make this Oregon angling classic once again available. I only regret that I never got to meet Francis Ames. He was a passionate fisherman, and a generous one. I'm sure he would be pleased to know that another generation of Oregon anglers will have the opportunity to follow his footsteps across the Oregon Country.

Dan Casali

*This volume is dedicated to my wife,
Laurel, my outdoor companion from
tenting to trailer days.*

INTRODUCTION

It was one of those January days such as only the normally mild-weathered Oregon coast can occasionally provide—drizzling rain, a raw wind off the Pacific, and cold, a penetrating, bone-chilling cold that turned fingers into clumsy, feelingless things. A man soon passed from the shivering stage into a sort of numb, hopeless misery. And the fishing was poor. It was as poor as only winter steelhead fishing can be at times, the slowest of the slow.

My two companions, Cliff Lemire, of Hebo, Oregon, and the author of this book, had long since become an unhealthy blue color. About eleven o'clock, after four frigid and fishless hours, Lemire said, "I've got to go to town and pick up some groceries. Do you want to go along?"

I assented quickly. By this time I would rather be anywhere than casting hopelessly to frozen or non-existent fish. The thought of the car's heater pouring blessed warmth over me was more enticing than the promise of heaven. The third member of our party said, "No, I'll stay."

Lemire and I drove to the little town down the river. We bought a loaf of bread and a pound of butter and then, partly because it was convenient, but mostly because we simply didn't have the guts to hurry back to the rushing, ice-cold river and stand in it in the drizzling rain, we crossed the street to Joe's beanery. There we drank quarts of coffee and let the heat of Joe's glowing stove soak us to the marrow.

At last there was no excuse to linger longer. We reluctantly went out into the rain and drove back to the river. There we found our companion attempting to wipe the icy water off his hands on his streaming boots. He had just finished dressing out an eighteen-pound steelhead, which he had landed a few minutes before. He was the picture of well-being. He glowed. Obviously, he felt neither the rain nor the ice-cold water in which his hands had been recently submerged.

This man was Francis H. Ames. I have fished with him. I have made coffee with him under the shelter of a thick-branched spruce while the rain came down. I have spread my bedroll beside his, eaten his food, I know him.

If anybody is qualified to write about fishing in Oregon, that man is Francis H. Ames. This volume tells what he knows—and nobody knows the subject better. Good fishing!

Ted Trueblood

AUTHOR'S PREFACE

My primary purpose in writing this book is to make it possible for readers to fish the Oregon country successfully during any month of the year. In undertaking this task I find myself in the precarious position of the angler who, when fishing for trout with a light leader, suddenly finds himself engaged with a forty-pound Chinook salmon. The fellow has the choice of giving up at once, or fighting it out to the bitter but very interesting end. I have chosen to take the latter course and so set my hand to the job with determination. If, in the course of these pages, I should snap the nylon in confusion, I ask my readers to remember that I did my best.

Certainly presenting the overall picture of angling in Oregon is a vast undertaking. The state contains over ninety-six thousand square miles of seacoast, mountain, valley, plain, and desert, threaded with countless streams and dotted with nearly a thousand lakes. It is patently impossible to cover all subjects in minute detail. There will be much that cannot be written in a single volume. I will present, however, the general why, where, and how of it.

After thirty-odd years of rather continuous fishing, hiking, hunting, and camping in Oregon, and eighteen years of writing about these experiences, I have come to the conclusion that whatever my limitations may be, I still may be able to save those who follow my trail a great deal of time and effort. The information contained in this book would have been highly appreciated when I first started fishing the Oregon country in 1923. Had I then possessed even a fraction of the inside information that I hope to put into this volume, those first angling years would have been far more pleasant and productive than they were. Since a great measure of what I know about Oregon angling was obtained through the kind offices of companions met streamside, I feel that I have an obligation to pass on to others what was so generously given to me.

Although my main purpose is to bring fish to the creel, I hope to be able to bring something more to my readers than meat to the pan, even as there is far more to angling than fish. There is the booming of the surf along Oregon beaches, and fog streamers drifting in the passes of the Coast Range at dawn when steelhead leap in the riffles. There is the breaking of spring in the Willamette Valley, the scent of pine along the shoulders of the Cascades, the heady atmosphere of the high desert, the silence of the canyons of the Rogue. These play an important part in the adventure of angling, be the creel light or heavy. So now we get on with it.

FISHING THE
OREGON COUNTRY

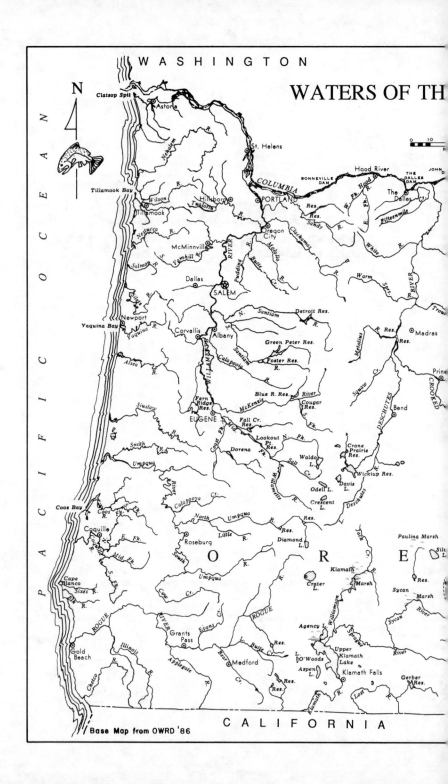

WASHINGTON

WATERS OF TH

PACIFIC OCEAN

OREGON

CALIFORNIA

Base Map from OWRD '86

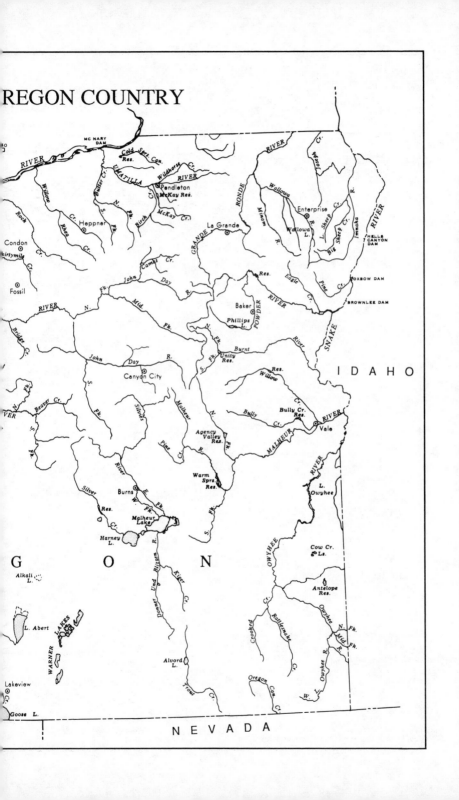

REGON COUNTRY

OREGON
COUNTRY OVERVIEW

THE OREGON COUNTRY IS A VAST AREA of incredible variety. From the flat lowland expanse of the populous Willamette Valley you can drive the points of the compass for hours.

Head east and you'll enter towering fir forests, and ascend the Cascade Range in the shadow of silent, glacier-capped volcanoes that stand two miles above the sea. Beyond the Cascades stretch high desert flats carpeted with with juniper and sage, slashed by deep whitewater river canyons. Even further east sprawl the pine covered Blue Mountains and the majestic alps-like Wallowas.

Tend southeast and you'll find range and basin country—isolated mountains with breathtaking rims, salt flats, and a remoteness Easterners can only dream about.

Head north and you'll meet the mighty Columbia River, a mile wide highway for steelhead and salmon to travel a thousand miles inland.

Head west and you'll be greeted by the deep green forests of the Coast Range mountains. Their diminished peaks of less than three thousand feet are sufficient to brunt the wrath of Pacific storms, which deluge the western slopes with as much as 120 inches of rain annually. Further west, the rocky headlands of the continent challenge crashing Pacific combers, while just inland stretch sweetwater lakes and misty river valleys which pasture Oregon's famous dairies.

With this much variety of terrain and climate, there is *always* good fishing *somewhere* in the Oregon country. To take full advantage of these opportunities, an angler should possess a sound working knowledge of Oregon's general topography. This is important both for the resident angler who would like to fish the year around, and for the vacationing fisherman who wants to make the most of limited time available. If the fishing is off where you are, some other section may well be offering the best fishing of the year.

For angling purposes I will subdivide the state into four sections, each of which presents unique opportunities and challenges. These are the **Oregon coast** (that area of the state extending from the Columbia River south to the California line, between the summit of the Coast Range Mountains and the Pacific Ocean); the **mid-valley** (that area extending south from the Columbia River to the valleys of the Rogue and Umpqua rivers, between the summits of the Coast Range and the Cascade Mountains); **eastern and central Oregon** (that vast area east of the Cascade summit all the way

2

to Idaho, and south to where the country breaks over into the Klamath Falls area) and **southern Oregon** (that area, drained by the Rogue, Umpqua, Illinois and Applegate rivers).

Each of these geographical divisions presents a unique face to the angler. Varied climates, altitudes, precipitation, insect activity, types of water, and available fish species suggest attention to this area or that at different times of the year. Trout fishing may be good in the mid-valley area when it is also good in eastern and central Oregon. Eastern and central Oregon may be at their best when some really intriguing angling is developing on the rivers of the coastal strip. Bass and panfish anglers may be having a fishing riot in the mid-valley section when they might be filling the creel with trout elsewhere. Frequently we are offered a variety of choices at a given moment. Let us take a quick look at the four angling areas.

Mid-valley

The Willamette Valley, running south from the Columbia River between the summits of the Coast Range and the Cascade Mountains, claims our attention first, since this region is at its best when trout season opens in the spring. This is a fairly heavily populated land with a dry summer climate and heavy winter rains, where snow seldom falls. The main streams of this region are the Columbia and the Willamette rivers and their numerous tributaries. There are also several lakes and many panfish sloughs.

Here we find native cutthroat trout, a deep-bodied, beautifully marked fish, together with rainbow trout which have been planted. Largemouth bass, crappie, bluegill, yellow perch and catfish offer sport for panfish anglers. There are limited numbers of smallmouth bass in the waters of the Willamette River below Eugene.

Steelhead trout, salmon, sturgeon, and shad are found in the Columbia, the Willamette, and in some tributaries, such as the Sandy, Clackamas, and Molalla rivers, both in spring and fall.

I generally hit the east-flowing valley waters early in spring, then move over to the west-flowing Cascade rivers in late May or when such a move is indicated by spring rains and water flow.

Since snowfall in the Coast Range Mountains is much lighter in winter than in the Cascades, streams flowing east out of the Coast Range into the Willamette Valley lose their volume and become less productive for trout earlier in the year. On the other hand, these same Coast Range streams lower and clear more quickly in spring, producing ideal trouting conditions earlier in the season. The east-flowing valley streams are comparatively short and heavily fished, as they are near the state's largest communities.

Coast Range streams that flow west into the Pacific Ocean are a different story. The coast gets more late spring rainfall than does the Willamette Valley. Consequently, west-flowing coastal waters are usually high and roiled when the season opens. They do attract numbers of trouters early in spring, but they are not, and never have been, good early trout streams, for reasons which I will discuss later.

Panfish seekers will continue to find plentiful catfish, bluegill, crappie, and largemouth bass in the lower slower reaches of the mid-valley streams, lakes, and sloughs throughout summer and fall.

Eastern and Central Oregon

When the eastern slopes of the high Cascades clear of snow in late May, I usually shift operations to eastern and central Oregon. Most high Cascade lakes are open to angling in late April, but such choice lakes as Paulina and East don't open until late May. Indeed, late April is too early to tackle many of these high-altitude waters, which are often ice bound into June.

Moving from the mid-valley area to eastern Oregon, the fisherman encounters quite different conditions. Ponderosa and jack pine replace fir and hemlock. The near sea level altitude of the mid-valley region climbs to typical altitudes of three to five thousand feet above sea level. There is a heady, piney scent to the air. The days are warmer, the nights nippier.

East from the forested slopes of the Cascades the land gives way to desert country. To the northeast lie the Blue and Wallowa mountains with their numerous streams and azure lakes. This is a vast, wonderful country for the outdoorsman.

Within this area flows the world-famed Deschutes River, which heads in the Cascades south of Bend among scores of mile high mountain lakes. Flowing from south to north, the Deschutes carves a canyon over a thousand feet deep through massive basalt on its hundred mile journey to the Columbia.

Cutthroat trout, which were most numerous in the mid-valley region, are infrequently found in these eastern waters. The cutts have been displaced primarily by introduced rainbow, which thrive here. Eastern brook, German brown, Dolly Varden, lake mackinaw, and kokanee (landlocked sockeye salmon) can all be found as well.

There is much greater insect activity here than in the mid-valley. Though all types of lures and bait can be used, the fly fisherman comes into his own in this region. Here, too, the wise angler brings a boat to launch on the many lakes where rentals are unavailable. Good fishing can be enjoyed in this area from May through summer and fall. Fall angling is often best here, right up until the trouting season closes in October.

However, I usually desert this area in August, moving west to fish the coastal rivers, which begin to offer attractions that I cannot resist. An angler can, of course, skip back and forth at this time between the two areas, such trips being a matter of three or four hours' driving over fast highways. I always plan to do this, but I become so involved on the coast streams that I seldom find time for more than one or two trips to eastern Oregon after August.

Oregon Coast

The Oregon coast is a long narrow strip, accessible throughout its length by highway 101. It is generally mountainous and forested, with fertile valleys along the lower portions of the major streams. Great bays and broad tidewaters jut inland, hiding their white water sources from the eyes of highway travelers. Forest roads, some of them paved, lead up every one of these streams, making them accessible to fishermen.

These rivers are famed for their runs of salmon, sea-run cutthroat, and steelhead (sea-run rainbow trout) in fall and winter. Salmon angling in coastal rivers usually begins in September. The steelhead runs start in November, continuing through March. I hit the coastal streams in August in order to be on hand when the sea-run cutthroat begin moving in, and the jack salmon start cavorting in tidewater.

The harvest trout, or sea-run cutthroat, is a marvelous fish, either for sport or for table use. In August, returning from the sea, these trout are fat, pink-meated, silver-bright—the best-eating trout in Oregon. They range from twelve to twenty-four inches long and provide top sport on bait, hardware, or fly. I should mention here, to avoid catcalls from the few veteran anglers who know about this, that there are runs of prime, upstream migrating sea-run cutthroat in some coastal streams in spring. These fish are sparse, hard to find, and not for the angler who does not know them well.

As much as I admire the fall-run harvest trout, this acrobatic battler is not my main reason for turning away from eastern Oregon fishing in August. I journey to the coast at this time of year for the jack salmon fishing. Jack salmon should be a favorite of summer trout fishermen, yet strangely few tackle these red-meated baby salmon. The jack salmon is not well known even to the average resident angler. We will fully discuss the secrets of jack salmon fishing in another chapter.

There are also many lakes along the coast which offer panfish, trout, and even sturgeon. Siltcoos Lake, below Florence, produces the largest black bass found this far north. Rivers in the Coos Bay area afford angling for striped bass and shad. Saltwater bays produce a bountiful variety of species. Casting into the sea from rocky headlands and sandy beaches might net sea perch, flounder, ling and rock cod, sea trout, red snapper, or sea bass. Clams can be dug in many areas, and luscious crabs can be taken with traps that are available for rent at docks and coastal sporting goods stores.

Southern Oregon

Southern Oregon is home to two of the most famous fishing streams in the West, the Rogue and the Umpqua. Unique among Oregon's coastal rivers, these draw from heavy alpine Cascade snows, penetrate the Coast Range, and flow to the sea. Because they head in the Cascades, they hold sufficient summer flow volume to support summer runs of anadromous fish, including sea-run cutthroat trout, salmon, and steelhead.

Both the Umpqua and Rogue offer spring fishing for salmon as early as March, with the best salmon months being April, May, and June. Steelhead also run in spring, reaching the upper river in August as a rule, affording some of the finest steelhead fly angling in Oregon. Both coho and chinook salmon enter these rivers in fall, starting in August and peaking in October.

I have fished both streams considerably, and I lived on the Rogue for three years, fishing it practically every day. I love it for sea-run fish, but I did not find it to be a particularly good trout stream. The best trouting on both the Rogue and the Umpqua is found in their higher reaches in the mountains. Actually, I enjoyed much better fly fishing for trout on the Rogue's middle and south forks than I did on the main stream. Two major tributaries of the Rogue, the Applegate and the Illinois, should not be overlooked for sea-run species and resident trout.

TROUTING
THE VALLEY STREAMS

I FIRST STARTED FISHING THE MID-VALLEY STREAMS while
on a two-week vacation in August of 1926, having driven
a thousand miles from southern California to reach
them. Had I the slightest knowledge of the state's fishing peculiarities, I would not have wasted my valuable
vacation days on streams flowing east from the Coast
Range in August.

The water was low and clear, and by scrambling
around in the brush and brambles from daylight until
dark, I managed to take a few fair size native cutthroat
trout, but each fish was well earned.

Looking back now, I realize that I could have taken

9

harvest trout in numbers at this time of year, and hooked jack salmon that would have strained my rod had I moved a few miles over the Coast Range Mountains to the coastal rivers. I could have found much better trouting by journeying across the valley to the Cascade streams, and had really wonderful fishing by topping the Cascade summit to hit eastern Oregon waters.

I mention this to stress the importance of knowing the general topography of the state, to avoid fishing at the wrong place at the wrong time of year. If I hadn't been a fool for punishment I might well have declared Oregon trouting to be a washout. Instead, I returned the next spring to fish these same waters again.

On my first venture the next spring I was accompanied by my older brother Lewis, an Oregon resident for a number of years. We opened the trout season on the North Fork of the Yamhill River, a couple of miles below the tiny town of Pike. I was astonished to discover that pools and runs which had defeated me the previous August now produced native cutthroat to sixteen-inches, fat, flossy, high-jumping acrobats. So much for inside information.

Mid-valley streams, for the most part, are trout streams only in those sections where they have fairly fast flow. The deep slow-flowing portions low in the valley are primarily panfish waters, home to bass, catfish, crappie, bluegill, and perch. Equipment for the trouting sections of these streams should always be either the fly or spinning rod, never the short bass-casting stick.

When the season opens in April these east-flowing mid-valley streams are usually too high and muddy for fly fishing. I have taken trout with deep drifted nymphs at this time of year, but bait is best. Drifting angle-worms with a single split shot for weight produces well, and I sometimes employ this technique, but I much

We opened the trout season on the North Fork of the Yamhill River.

prefer to use a baited spinner at this time. Small spinning rod plugs, spoons, and spinners work well here, but the deadliest lure on these native cutthroat trout is the six-inch double-bladed spinner, such as the Indiana or Doc Shelton, with chrome and brass finish, followed by an angleworm strung on a six-inch leader and number eight hook.

As for techniques, it is useless to cast a double spinner rig out and draw it toward you. A peculiarity of the trout in these east-flowing valley waters is that they refuse to hit a lure that is being drawn upstream toward the angler. They take it as it is easing downstream, or when it is held in one place in the current and woven back and forth.

The proper technique is to wade out to the main thread of water flow above a pool or run. If the water is too swift or deep to be reached by wading, reach out with the rod tip so that it is directly above the main line of flow. Now drop it down a few more feet to repeat the process. Continue this until you get a strike. Take careful note of where this strike occurred. Mentally place it by a portion of the bank or a noticeable current thread or boil. This is very important.

Once you have located an area where trout strike in a given pool or run you will find that they will strike at this identical spot year after year, unless the stream bed changes so radically that current threads and bottom structure alter. These *hot spots* are generally not over five or six feet long. Quite often there are three or four such striking spots in a given pool or run, though at times you may find only one, or none. After you have located these places on one of the mid-valley streams you hold a pat hand, often for years.

Using the double-bladed baited spinner, I soon discovered that the length of the leader between hook and spinner was very important. Quite often it is the seemingly insignificant things that count in fishing, as I found one spring, when my brother and I fished the green pasturelands below Pike on the North Fork of the Yamhill on opening day of trout season.

Fishing was simply wonderful that day. We hooked cutthroats to seventeen inches, broad beamed, beautifully marked fish that turned somersaults all over the place. For reasons we did not discover until later, I landed a large percentage of the trout I hooked, while Lewis lost most of his in the play. This exasperated him no end.

It appeared that he just couldn't hold onto his fish to bring them to creel. After considerable study of the matter we came to the conclusion that he had lost his fish because his snell, between hook and spinner, was an inch or more shorter than mine. His trout, though attracted to the whirling spinner blades, feared them. They were striking at the worm but were striking short. This tended to hook them lightly.

Over a period of years I experimented with various snell lengths between spinner and hook. I have watched from high banks and bridges as trout struck at bait that followed spinners, noting that the fish approached with terrific speed, yet seemed to switch into reverse even as they struck. Attracted to the bait by the spinner, nevertheless they struck as if fearing to draw any nearer the blades than necessary. I found that the longer the snell between spinner and hook, the lighter the strike and the deeper the hooking; the shorter the snell, the more savage the strike and the shallower the hooking. For hard, solid, jolting strikes with secure hooking, the six-inch leader works out well. Against such a rig in fast water, a trout of any size brings a thrilling punch to the rod.

Spinner fishing with bait requires great skill in judgement of water, wading, and the handling of the lure. No fly purist should look down upon the man skilled in this technique. When I first attempted it I was

13

a fly purist and inclined to believe that this was but a fumbling game. Make no mistake about it, fishing the baited spinner in fast streams is an art, an art in angling being any technique with which one person can take fish while another cannot. I have had quite a bit of fun proving this premise to companions.

In the spring of 1939 I took George Curtright, a husky son of a local chicken rancher, out on the Yamhill to introduce him to spinner and worm fishing. He went down the stream ahead of me, out of my sight. An hour or so later I came up with him, my creel heavy. I found him standing by a pool where a swift current came boiling down in a curve. He was fishless and very discouraged.

"I don't believe that there's a trout in this crick," he declared.

"I'll bet," I told him, "that there's trout right in front of you. This is one of the best runs in the stream."

I flipped the baited spinner out, let it down a ways, wove it back and forth. A beautifully marked twelve-inch cutthroat smashed it on the first pass.

I have introduced many anglers to this method of trouting and have yet to encounter one who could master it without considerable trial and error. Strong current flow is necessary for this technique. Since currents are strong in east-flowing mid-valley streams only in early spring, this method must be discontinued later in the season. Then one should turn to drifted bait, or to flies. Effective flies include the Black Gnat (Grey Hackle Yellow), Light and Dark Cahill, and March Brown, in sizes ten and twelve.

Using flies, it is well to know the secret of the suckers. Many of these waters have large runs of spawning suckers in spring. There is a particularly heavy run in the North Fork of the Yamhill River near McMinnville. When suckers can be seen schooled in the lower reaches of pools and runs, fish the riffles below them for trout

14

which will be lying below, feeding on sucker roe. As I write in August of 1965, Carlton Lake is being drained, so that a new dam can be built to replace the old one. The lake will be deepened and restocked. This should improve trout fishing in the North Fork of the Yamhill, into which Carlton Lake trout migrate in spring. Strangely enough, although trout below spawning suckers are feeding on tapioca-shaped roe, they will only take dry flies avidly at this time.

An amusing incident in this connection occurred one evening at a meeting of the Yamhill County Sportsmen's Association, of which I have long been a member. A fellow member rose from his seat to protest about the run of suckers up the Yamhill, declaring that they should be eliminated, and that because of them there were no longer any trout in this water. Moon Mullins, then the Yamhill County Federal trapper, came to his feet to reply to this.

"Well, now," he declared smacking his lips, "I just got through eating a fine mess of trout that Ames dropped off at my house, and he had a few more in his basket. Got 'em on the Yamhill, he did, fishing right below those spawning suckers."

I really had a time that year fishing flies below those suckers in a drift beside the abandoned rock crusher, some two miles below Pike. I fished this pool once or twice a week, with the barb flattened on my hooks, releasing most of the fish taken. I had no way of knowing if I was taking the same fish over and over again, but the supply seemed endless.

Any valley stream with a run of spawning suckers is apt to be a good trout stream in spring. Suckers don't interfere with trout, but trout do get fat and sassy on sucker roe and on sucker fingerlings emerging from the gravel. I won't say that suckers won't interfere with trout in some waters where they are resident, but I do maintain that they are an asset when they just come up on a spawning visit.

15

If I were to intimate that trout fishing is as good today in these east-flowing valley streams as it was when I first fished them in 1926, or even as good as it was in 1955, I would be deceiving my readers. It definitely is not. But there are still a good many native cutthroat which have retained their belligerent attitude toward bait, spinner, or fly.

Large spawner cutthroat move up from the Columbia into the Willamette, and thence into the various Willamette tributaries, restocking these waters. Every year in September, for instance, many large cutthroat are taken below the main Yamhill locks at Lafayette. Had these fish escaped the hook, and many of these migratory cutthroat do, they would have proceeded on up the north and south forks of the Yamhill and into their tributaries.

On any Oregon stream, never take it for granted that there are no trout in front of you just because you aren't taking them. Chances are they are there but are just not hitting, or they require a different lure or technique than you are using at the moment. The mood of the fish quite often holds the answer, as I found out one day when fishing the Willamina above the town of that name.

I had been fishing for hours without a strike. The late spring day was hot and windless. Arm-weary and boot sore, I sat down on a sandbar in the shade. It was very relaxing sitting there, listening to the song of the stream, the twittering of the birds in the alders. I soon fell asleep. When I awakened with a start, dusk was fast coming down. Moving toward my car, I began casting as I went, not expecting any results.

Man, that stream had suddenly turned as hot as a two-dollar pistol! I nailed into wallopers that blew gravel into the air with their acrobatics. These fish were wild and eager, striking in the very same water that had appeared barren a few hours previously. Changing to flies, as I always do when fish are striking well at dusk, I drifted a Black Gnat through a narrow pocket where I had never been able to take a sizable trout, and laced into a seventeen-inch cutthroat. Mind you, I wasn't even attempting to fish the tiny pocket of water, a split-off from the main stream. I just tossed my fly on its surface to keep it free of the brush as I edged around the spot. When that scrapper blew up beneath the Black Gnat I could hardly believe it. But there he was, fat and frisky.

The biggest trout of the stream were cruising about in the shallow riffles at the foot of pools and runs. When they blasted a floating fly, water flew in all directions. Except for my drifting off into slumber, I might have gone home missing one of the fastest fishing experiences of my life.

The mood of the moment is always a factor with trout, but I am inclined to think that mood enters into the picture of these valley streams even more than is usual. I can tell within a matter of minutes what my fortune will be on these streams during the next hour or so. Sometimes the water seems to be devoid of trout. At other times only small trout will hit. However, if you take a big one right away, you can gamble that big ones are striking all over the stream. A fisherman learns to sense such things.

I will not attempt to name all the valley streams flowing east from the Coast Range, if, indeed I could name them all. Your detailed maps will show them. My favorites are the North Fork of the Yamhill, a mile above Pike and two miles below; the South Fork of the Yamhill, near Valley Junction; the Willamina, out of Willamina; Baker Creek, west from McMinnville; Panther Creek, west from Carlton; Agency Creek at Old Grande Ronde; and the Luckiamute, near Corvallis.

During recent years hatchery rainbow trout have been dumped into these east-flowing valley streams.

The dumps are usually made quite high in the foothills. This has attracted a great number of anglers to the higher waters. Personally, I don't care to follow the fish dump truck, or to take newly deposited hatchery trout. The best trouting for good size wild trout is in the lower reaches of these streams, between their mountain headwaters and the point where the flow slows upon reaching the level valley.

Turning from the east-flowing streams of the mid-valley to those which flow west from the Cascades, we have a different picture. Here we have rivers which hold their flow better in late spring and summer. We have fewer cutthroat, more rainbow, some Dolly Varden, and in the famous McKenzie, that most prized of trout, the redside, a variant of the rainbow. We find more insect activity here and so have better fly fishing.

The main west-flowing streams are the Sandy, at Troutdale; the Clackamas, east of Oregon City; the Molalla, near Molalla; the North Santiam, running along Highway 22 east from Salem; the South Santiam, along Highway 20; the headwaters of the Willamette, in the Oakridge area along Highway 58; and the gorgeous McKenzie.

A study of detailed maps will disclose that there are many tributaries of these rivers which are worthy of attention. Anglers who know their business will find good trouting in the more heavily fished waters of the better known streams. But there are stretches of these rivers that are overlooked by the multitudes, and that a fisherman can locate with a little effort and a good map. I must confess, however, that the success Clark Bond and I had one Fourth of July came about by accident rather than design.

On the Fourth of July a few years back, Eugene sportsman Clark Bond accompanied me on a trip along the North Santiam. We had been out three days fishing the McKenzie and other adjacent waters and were on our way home. We had been wading all day and were a bit weary as we drove along the Santiam at dusk. Since we had a complete camp outfit with us, we began looking for a place to park for the night. Bond threw the wheel hard over to enter a barely discernible trace, where overhanging brush lashed at the windshield.

We emerged in a tiny clearing on the banks of the north fork of the Santiam, hardly fifty yards from the highway. Rolling out our sleeping bags, we bedded down to the song of the river. I awakened at dawn and reached for my camera to photograph a doe deer with two fawns at her side. After breakfast we prepared to fish.

We were quite close to the summit of the Cascades here. The Santiam, which becomes a broad river below, was scarcely twenty feet wide at this point, clear as crystal over white sand and gravel. Tossing bait, spinner, or plug here would only frighten any trout that might be present. Using dry flies in size twelve and fourteen, with nine-foot leaders tapered to 2X, we took several plump rainbow without moving out of camp. Though Fourth of July fisherfolk were out in numbers, we didn't meet another angler all day.

The use of small flies on light terminal gear was plainly indicated here, but I recall a time when the trout of this stream had me baffled for the better part of a day. Floyd Curtright of Jacksonville and his son, George, accompanied me on this trip to the North Santiam in June. We fished a few miles below where Bond and I filled our creels. The river was larger here, with stronger flow, but very clear. I worked the water hard that day, without result. It seemed to me that there were no trout present.

Feeling in need of a smoke, I cast my dry fly across the stream, tucking the rod beneath my arm as I broke out cigarette and lighter. As I was doing this the fly floated down, drifting into an almost still eddy. It danced there for long moments over a sandy bottom so clearly visible that one could have read a newspaper lying on the sand. With flame cupped to my cigarette, I saw a husky rainbow slowly rising beneath the fly. It was an astonishing thing. The fish had simply materialized. There seemed no way that it could have arrived beneath the fly without my observing its approach.

The rainbow inhaled the fly, then leisurely turned to go down. Cigarette flew one way, lighter the other as I frantically tried to set the hook. Meanwhile, the trout rejected the artificial and disappeared. This occurrence was the tip-off. I began to let my flies drift into still eddies and lie there completely undisturbed. I took the best creel of good size rainbows that day that I have ever taken from the North Santiam.

Flies are seldom used by the great majority of Oregon anglers. This is the only state I have fished where this is the case. Flies actually require no more skill than bait or the various hardware artificials, such as spoons, spinners, plugs, and wobblers, though false claims to the contrary have long been a part of angling history. The point here is that deft handling of the fly is something which can be observed and admired, while the skillful manipulation of bait and hardware artificials is not so apparent. When conditions are at all right for flies, the feathers will take more fish per fishing hour than any other lure. Sometimes, if flies are used by a master in the art, they will also pay off when conditions are not at all right.

Several years ago, outdoor writer and fishing veteran Byron Dalrymple visited me. We fished the valley streams when the water was high and muddy. Using bait, spoons, and wobblers we got very thoroughly skunked. Then, since we were not taking trout anyway, we turned to flies merely for the fun of casting them. I was considerably astonished when a foot-long cutthroat suddenly bored up from the bottom to nail one of Byron's dry flies. He took several trout on dry flies before we both tied on brown nymphs, which produced even better. I believe that Oregon anglers would gain in sport if they would employ flies more often on our waters.

The McKenzie River, one of the west flowing Cascade streams, is fine fly water. There are more highly educated trout in the McKenzie than in any other stream I have fished. One time, when moving down the McKenzie, I encountered a couple who called me to come see some really smart trout. These anglers were casting spinners into the drink and reeling them back. Several gorgeous rainbows followed the moving lures. These trout were following the spinner in so close to shore that we could see them in the clear water. When the fish were in close, the man would cast a tiny hook, baited with a single salmon egg strung on a leader of two-pound breaking strength. The trout ignored this, yet would instantly take a salmon egg floating freely. This proved that the leader itself, as fine as it was, warned these fish. And yet these same trout took my flies when cast on the same breaking strength leader.

This points out why flies are so successful on wary trout. A fish has time to look over a slowly sinking bait, or one drawn behind a spinner. But it seems to feel that it must strike fast and without hesitation at an insect, which may fly away at any moment. These trout, which we could see, teach us never to feel that waters where we are failing are barren of trout. Trout we cannot see may well be just as wary as these McKenzie river fish were. To take them, perhaps, we need only change our fishing technique, or fine down our gear.

The McKenzie River, which heads in Clear Lake, off Highway 126 above Blue River, possesses the most beautifully hued water in the world. At the witching hour of dusk pastel shades of green, blue, violet, and lavender flicker in its falls and rapids. Some of the deeper runs take on shades of green and brilliant purple.

Below the falls in one spot a huge trout leaps every evening at dusk. I have been trying in July for several seasons to take this trout. It leaps at the very edge of the falls, across the stream, at a point impossible to reach by wading. There is an extremely tricky fly casting problem to be solved here. Casting across the stream to the rise puts a roaring rapid between rod and the fly. These rapids pick up the belly of the line to sweep it downstream, which brings drag to the fly as soon as it lands.

This big trout is too smart to be fooled by a dragging fly. The technique to use in this situation is known as the "Lazy S cast." I wobble the rod tip back and forth widely as the cast goes forward. This drops the line on the water in a series of S loops. The current has to straighten out these loops before it can bring drag to the fly, and this gives the fly a few seconds of drag-free float. I have employed this cast many times on this big leaper of the McKenzie. I try my best to take the huge rainbow, but I confess to having mixed feelings about my failure, or my success. The McKenzie would not be the same without this jumping beauty.

Whether you use flies, artificial hardware, or bait on these mid-valley streams, there is a world of trouting here for enjoyment. A certain amount of skill is required in the use of each type of lure.

Modern spinning gear is ideal for handling bait and hardware on these fast trout streams. Use worms with a number eight bait holder hook of the Eagle Claw type. Use single salmon eggs on a number ten or eight short shanked salmon egg hook, which will permit the hook to be completely buried in the egg.

The clearer the water, the lighter and longer the leader should be. You may be able to hook valley stream trout on a leader of ten pound breaking strength in roiled water, but in clear it might require one or two pound breaking strength.

When drifting bait for any type of fast stream fish, and this includes both salmon and steelhead, the bait should be drifted slowly and close to the bottom. This makes the choice of sinker weight important. Split shot are ideal for this work. Carry along a pair of long-nosed pliers to attach shot to line. These pliers, with their long slim blades, are also essential for removing hooks from trout which you might want to release unharmed.

When clamping split shot onto a leader, be careful not to pinch so tightly that you injure the leader material; pinch just tight enough to hold the shot in position. Several small split shots are better than one or more larger shots, since the smaller lead is less inclined to hang up on bottom obstructions. A couple of air rifle sized shots are usually enough weight for bait on the valley streams.

With this rig, cast the bait across and at an angle upstream. Then let it drift on a fairly slack line until it makes a turn below you. Let it settle and lie a few moments before the retrieve. For unbaited spoons, spinners, plugs, and wobblers use this same technique. Even when the hardware artificial is not baited, try letting the artificial down from above and weaving it back and forth at intervals.

After you have taken some of these gorgeous valley stream trout, you will want to get them home to the frying pan in top condition. The best way to do this, I've found, is to nest them in the creel with green grass or leaves separating one fish from the other. This packing material should not be wet, just green. Wetness softens trout and prevents a protecting glaze from forming.

In a lifetime, no man could fish all the east and west-flowing valley streams enough to know them even fairly well. The man who knows all of them well does not exist. But no matter. One fair-sized trout stream known well, in all its moods, is a treasured jewel in an angler's crown.

A stream is not always loved best for its wealth of trout. Quite often it is a combination of factors that wins an angler's heart. Although the north fork of the Yamhill River below and above Pike is not nearly as productive for trout today as it was years back, it is still my favorite mid-valley trout stream for early spring fishing. I like it for its spring atmosphere. At this time all the world about is green and flowering. Deer and coon tracks imprint the sandbars. Each pool, riffle and run holds pleasant memories. Here an eighteen-incher broke a leader on the strike, and there, where that smooth dark water flows beneath the overhanging tree (that was but a shrub when I first saw it so long ago), I took that brilliantly spotted sixteen-incher that made six leaps in succession before being subdued. Memories, to me, are like gold coins in the bank.

Rivaling the North Fork of the Yamhill in my affections is the swift but placidly flowing Little Deschutes of the eastern Oregon country. Rolling down the east slope of the Cascade Mountains, winding through green cattle ranges, it is a beautiful stream to fish in June. It is equally beautiful in October in its autumn coloring and form. At dusk ducks wing overhead, silhouetted against a crimson sunset. At such times I am hard put to tell which stream I love best, but I do know that I am thankful to be alive, and a fisherman.

EAST OF THE CASCADES
FOR TROUT

FORTUNATE INDEED IS THE TROUT ANGLER who finds himself east of the Cascades in Oregon from June through October. From the Blue Mountains in the north to the Klamath Basin in the south, this is fishing country. Here flow the Big and Little Deschutes, the Crooked, Malheur, Powder, White, and Crescent rivers, to name a few of the many waters in this area. As one man prefers a blonde, another a brunette, a third a redhead, so do fishermen vary in their preference for trout streams.

In east-central Oregon the Big Deschutes, as distinguished from the Little Deschutes, is the favorite stream of more anglers than any other. However, the Little

Deschutes, flowing fast but quietly through green cattle ranges, is by far my favorite east-central Oregon water. I like this river for its fishing, and for its quiet pastoral setting.

My wife Laurel and I arrived on the banks of the Little Deschutes, ten miles south of Lapine, in June of 1962. We had fished this tributary of the Big Deschutes many times in the past, but had never hit it before at this particular spot. Here, a half mile above where it is joined by the Crescent, the Little Deschutes is narrow and brush choked, contrasting with its wide flow through open meadowlands below.

Standing on a narrow wooden bridge and looking downstream, we witnessed a sight which few anglers are ever privileged to see. German brown trout were feeding avidly on spent Mayflies. There were often several trout in the air at once. My fingers trembled as I strung my rod and pulled on waders.

On this occasion I decided to do a bit of showing off for my wife, to prove to her just how good I was. Several trout were feeding where the stream made a sharp bend below the bridge. The situation called for the utmost finesse. I carefully dressed a number 12 Blue Upright with oil, strung it on a nine-foot leader tapered to a pound and a half breaking strength, and cast it twenty feet above the rising fish. I waggled the rod to feed out line as the fly drifted, tensed for the strike.

The fly danced on the little riffles, floating high and beautifully. The rise came with lightning swiftness. I reacted to it with a wrist snap that popped the leader and flung the line into the trees. My wife was unable to keep a straight face. She giggled until she was weak as I climbed the tree to retrieve my line, red-necked with embarrassment.

When trout are rising like this I am inclined to become a bit unstrung, like a beagle when he gets his first sniff of rabbit. It takes a bit of doing to settle down, to get the old reflexes under control so that one can set a hook delicately with a spider web leader.

We had an exciting day on the Little Deschutes. Properly executed casts brought results, poor ones failure. These were not large trout, but they were beautifully colored specimens which measured from eight to twelve inches. Who could ask for more? But knowing brown trout as I do, I was not fooled by their size. I knew that larger fish must lurk in these waters, and that we were probably only taking the uneducated youngsters. The sequel to this came the following year when we visited this spot.

Again the browns were rising. But I noticed a peculiar thing. There were no trout rising at the bend of the river below the little bridge where rises had been most numerous the year before. I could see no change in the conformation of the stream that might cause this. It puzzled me, nagged at my mind as we fished through the day.

Might a really big brown have taken over this piece of water, a cannibalistic individual who had driven smaller fish away? With this thought in mind I sneaked back to the river bend at dusk. Oregon law does not permit night fishing for trout, but does permit angling until an hour after sunset. By then darkness is well advanced. I slipped up on the rapid at the tail of the pool, determined to make a perfect cast.

I knew the exact spot where, the year before, trout had been taking fallen insects as they broke over the tail of the pool. Cautiously I waded through the tall grass at the water's edge, stooped, head low. I stripped off line, made a single false cast, and then sailed the fly over the water, checking it high so that it would float down softly on the water.

A great mistake made by many flycasters is to whip the rod back and forth with multiple false casts as they strip out line. It is better to get closer to your chosen spot by stealthy stalking and to make a single backward false cast so that the line comes out over the water, and the wary trout, only once. On this momentous occasion my fly came to rest on the water as silently as thistle down, cocked prettily. It was the cast of my life.

I watched the fly drifting in the dusk. I held my breath, every nerve and muscle poised for the strike. When it came, it was a mere dimpling of the water as the fly disappeared. I lifted the tip and wrist-set the hook home. After that it was every man for himself.

I'm not quite sure what happened, what mistake I made in the play. All I know is that this brown was big and fast, and in the air more than he was in the water. I had him on for perhaps ten seconds, then he was gone. Ten seconds is a short time in a man's life, just long enough to pick up the phone when it rings, to wave to a neighbor, to slip on your shirt. Yet when ten seconds pass while you lose a big trout at dusk, you remember them vividly for as long as you live.

The tale of a trout lost, I realize, is not nearly as appetizing as is the tale of a trout landed. Two years previous to losing the big brown on the upper Little Deschutes, we fished several miles lower, also in June. Here the stream flows swiftly yet silently, without rapids or white water, winding through green cattle ranges where wild flowers bloom in profusion.

On this occasion I took several nice browns, the largest measuring nineteen inches. Again I noticed a rapid at the foot of a pool on a sharp river bend where there did not seem to be any trout, though there were trout in all other likely waters. In fact, this particular stretch of the river seemed ideal for trout.

I avoided the spot until dusk, then approached it cautiously. This time the big one took the lure deep, and fought with such power and determination that I labored up and down the bank for twenty minutes before bringing it to the net. I judged this brown to weigh over five pounds. A good trout, indeed, but rumor has it that a woman angler took a brown here that weighed fourteen pounds.

A skin diver who swam six miles of this river, observing the fish in their own element, reported seeing numerous large browns in the Little Deschutes. All you have to do is be smart enough to fool them. If these were rainbow or brook trout, cutthroat or Dolly Varden, I might undertake to tell how. But with German browns, who knows? When we get right down to the crux of the matter, it isn't the knowing how that counts so much as knowing that the fish are there for the taking. Few anglers would ask for more.

On browns you try a worm drifted deep, a high-floated fly, a craftily handled spoon or plug, and then you crawl around the meadow slapping down grasshoppers with your hat, and try them. Everything else failing, you sit down on the bank and ponder the matter. But when you finally lift a husky brown from the water, you are entitled to hold it high while you yell, "I am a fisherman!".

Although browns are found in the main Deschutes River and in some of the eastern Oregon lakes and streams, the Little Deschutes is the only strictly brown trout stream that I know of in the state. In years of fishing this beautiful river I have taken only two rainbow from it, and these recently. May the fellow who planted rainbow in the Little Deschutes have his neck caught in a wringer if, indeed, they were deliberately planted. Every land should have at least one brown trout stream. Browns may not leap as high as rainbows, but they require more angling skill than any other trout. When on a brown trout stream, I am always sure that there are fish before me, for these trout are too crafty, too quick to learn, to ever be fished out, as may happen with other species.

When considering fishing the area east of the Cascade summit for trout, most anglers think of the Big Deschutes, which is as famed in the West as the Beaverkill is in the East. I recall that I slept on the ground on the Big Deschutes for three nights one May, in weather that was a witch's brew of lightning, thunder, torrential rain, and snow, dished out with periods of sun and moonshine. At dawn I peered from my sleeping bag, overhung with a light canvas tarp, to see beaver going about their tree-cutting business in the mist that hung over the water. At night the clouds often parted permitting the full moon to shine. When this occurred, a million tiny frogs set up such a singing that a golden world vibrated to their music.

I took browns with deep-drifted night crawlers, rainbow with high-floated flies. I spent two hours taking one husky rainbow which was almost as thick as it was long. This rainbow presented a delicate problem for the dry fly, since it was rising between two logs that frothed with foam. I've waded the Big Deschutes below Bend, where rainbow rose over fine gravel, and fished it close to its confluence with the Columbia near The Dalles. But to me the most fascinating portion of this river is high in the mountains above Crane Prairie Reservoir east of Bend.

Here the Deschutes is but a mountain creek, ten to twenty feet wide, fast and ice-cold, clear as crystal. It flows through high mountain meadows sprinkled with an amazing variety of wild flowers. Here one often encounters mule deer and elk. Snowcapped peaks are always in view, even in midsummer. The air is like wine, and the trout are more brilliantly hued than they are anywhere else. There are large, acrobatic rainbow here if you have the skill to take them. One of the secrets of this section of the Big Deschutes, which I have guarded quite jealously for some time, is that in mid-June both rainbow and eastern brook run up into the stream from Crane Prairie.

Here the Deschutes is but a mountain creek.

Another of my secrets here is that the really big eastern brook trout from Crane Prairie only go up the Deschutes as far as Snow Creek. For some reason known only to the brooks, they turn off into this tiny stream that flows through dense timber and downed slash, obstructed here and there by beaver dams.

It pains me to do so, but I'll go one step farther in disclosing my inside information on this section of the Deschutes. To take the big brooks which turn aside into Snow Creek you must use a dark streamer fly, weighted so that it can be drifted beneath logs and other slash. Dark threads of moss waving in crystal clear water close to the sandy bottom may hide an eastern brook as long as your arm from elbow to fingertips.

Brooks which are resident in the upper Deschutes and Snow Creek are small, but firm as iced butter, black-sided with brilliant red dots. The only other spot where I have found such highly colored brooks was in a tiny trickle in the California Sierras, between Lake Tahoe and Truckee, which I located with a Forest Service map.

Read your maps of the Deschutes River country, of the Wallowas and Blue Mountains, then turn to the eastern desert country. Surprisingly, there are many streams flowing through Oregon's deserts, some of them seldom fished. They flow through sand and sage, where the air is heady with the scent of sun-cured juniper. Take a look down Silver Lake way, where I have fished two desert streams that hold surprises for the adventurous angler.

Silver Creek flows across Highway 31, hardly two hundred yards from the town of Silver Lake. Buck Creek crosses this same highway, about two miles north and west of Silver Lake. Turn south and east from the highway on a dirt road to strike Silver Creek, still within hearing distance of the highway. Here is fishing with a fly cast on a short line.

I discovered Silver Creek quite by accident. I had a date to meet John Cowles of Rainier, Oregon, at the town of Silver Lake. John, in addition to being a very able nature photographer, is a real enthusiast of Indian lore and artifacts. In the desert, he had discovered a water hole that never went dry, a rather surprising discovery in a land where water holes are conspicuous by their absence.

Around this water hole John had found evidence indicating that this had once been a favored gathering place for the early Indian tribes, Indians who were here when the world was young. Indian writings on the rock walls around the water hole were thought to be more than ten thousand years old. John and his party had decided to take in a gasoline-powered pump to drain the water hole so they could dig in its bottom for artifacts. I was invited to take part in this expedition.

Unknown to me, John had broken an ankle and was delayed. As I had time on my hands, I consulted my detailed map of the area and located a stream that I had previously driven past without even noticing. I drove back, turned down the dirt road, and parked beside blue water. By the time I had my rod strung I had seen several rises. Though I have been informed that there are eastern brooks here, all the fish I took were rainbow, ranging from small to a top of ten inches. An old-timer of the area told me later that, had I moved downstream a mile or so, I might have taken rainbow to three or four pounds.

I also drove up Buck Canyon to fish Buck Creek. This is fascinating country, where juniper trees stand so thick in the butt that they must be hundreds of years old. Mule deer tracks are everywhere, and as I approached the stream I jumped a four pointer from his bed in the shade of a boulder, his antlers still in the moss. Buck Creek is but a tiny trickle at this time of year, and should be fished earlier. I did take a few pan-sized trout by cautious handling of a dry fly. John Cowles treasures the Indian artifacts we took from the water hole; I treasure my rocking-chair memories of fishing desert streams in July.

Another instance where the maps showed us trout in desert country came about when my wife and I were deer hunting at the foot of Walker Rim, east of Chemult. The year had been extremely dry. The deer were hard to find, so we cruised about in search of fresh deer tracks. I reasoned that deer would be where there was water. The map of the area showed that there was a small stream, named Miller Creek, flowing across Highway 97 about ten miles south of Chemult.

I had driven this route many times without realizing that this trickle was there. We drove down the highway, located the stream and, turning west on a dirt trace, followed it into the forest. We found deer tracks in plenty, but we also found trout. The fish hung in water so clear that they seemed to be painted in glass. We didn't fish for them because we were too busy with our deer. But we'll be back.

Locating streams that the other fellow doesn't know about is a real experience, even if the trout found aren't so large that they hang over the edge of the frying pan. Discovery always has been intriguing to outdoor folks. Speaking of discovery, rumor has it, and my maps confirm, that tiny Miller Creek flows into a large beaver dam marsh where there has been fabulous fishing for big rainbow at certain times of the year. All over the Oregon country, discovery and adventure await the fisherman who ventures beyond well-known waters.

One of the most intriguing fishing stories I have ever read was written by a Portland nature photographer for *Field and Stream*, about fishing the Kiger River of Steens Mountain in southeastern Oregon. This fellow set a lantern outside his tent at night and gathered the white millers that were attracted to the light. Using these tiny insets for bait at dawn, he took a string of rainbow which I have been dreaming about ever since I read the account.

Driving the forest roads which lead to the high lakes of the Deschutes River drainage, one crosses many rushing, ice cold trout streams. Most of these waters are open for angling during trout season, but should not be fished without first consulting a booklet of Oregon angling laws. My wife and I crossed many of these streams when we covered fourteen high mountain lakes on a writing assignment for *Outdoor Life*.

I don't want to harp on the use of flies, for I am not by any means a fly purist, but the way to fish these small creeks is with flies. They are swarming with tiny trout, in addition to the big ones, which any angler worthy of his rod would want to release uninjured. Bait is usually taken deep, but trout taken in fast water with flies are usually hooked in the lips. This permits release without harm.

Many fishermen give up fly fishing after a few attempts. After they wind the fly line around their necks a few times, hang it up in the brush, and beat the water enough to frighten every trout in the pool, they take it for granted that they are too awkward to learn the game, or that learning would be too difficult. In my experience, it is most often a crudely balanced outfit that brings about discouragement, rather than any lack of native skill on the part of the fisherman. It is a fact that it is practically impossible to lay down a fly skillfully with a badly put together fly rig, and very easy to do so with properly balanced gear. Today, with lines made of all sorts of materials, with the floater weighing much less than the sinker, with double tapers and forward tapers or torpedoes, about the only way the amateur flycaster can get a line balanced is to consult an expert who will take the outfit in his hand to judge its feel.

A line must be heavy enough to pull the rod tip back on the back cast, to bring the rod into action, and yet not too heavy. However, one item of fly rod equipment remains constant. This is the taper of the leader. No matter how delicately balanced the line and rod may be as a unit, it will not put a fly down on the water properly unless the leader has the proper taper.

I have had some of my most enjoyable trouting days, sampling the wild streams which flow along the eastern shoulders of the Cascade Mountains. There is fascination in these clear, ice-cold brooks, regardless of the trout taken. Fortune in using flies on these high latitude eastern-central Oregon streams is dependent on insect activity, weather conditions, and clarity of the water. Far more trout are taken here on bait and hardware artificials than are caught on flies, even by anglers who are adept with the feathers.

The same techniques with bait and hardware work here as were recommended for the mid-valley streams, except that rainbow of the high country will hit a faster moving bait than will cutthroat in the lower altitudes. The German browns here are, in my opinion, the best fly-taking trout of the area. Nevertheless, when the water is high and roiled, bait is the ticket for browns, especially the larger specimens.

When drifting bait for browns, drift it slowly and close to the bottom, for these red and yellow spotted beauties hit hesitantly on bait. They prefer large bait, such as a whole nightcrawler. Thread the forward end of the worm on a number eight bait hook so that the hook will be entirely concealed, leaving the tail of the long worm free to wiggle behind. Cast across and upstream; allow a slow drift and a lie in deep water at the end of the drift. Always give slack line when you sense the beginning of the strike, delaying several seconds before setting the hook.

Stream fishing for trout is my favorite pastime. My boyhood on a Montana ranch, where there was no running water of any kind, and where the only shade was that afforded by a barbed-wire fence, has made me appreciate streams which run clear and musical over clean gravel. This feeling of appreciation has grown through the years. Fast mountain streams are my first love. My second are blue lakes tucked away in green forests. The Oregon country holds many such lakes. Let's have a look at some of them.

FISHING
THE HIGH LAKES

SCATTERED THROUGHOUT THE MOUNTAIN RANGES of the Oregon country–among the lofty peaks and valleys of the Cascade Range, the jagged granite Wallowas, the Blues and Coast Range mountains–there are more lakes than you can shake a piscatorial stick at in a couple of ordinary lifetimes.

These mountain beauties offer fabulous fishing for rainbow, eastern brook, Dolly Varden, mackinaw or lake trout, and German browns. There are also some cutthroat trout and the acrobatic landlocked sockeye salmon, called kokanee or *blueback*.

Some of the high lakes are small and seldom fished. In fact, many can only be reached by foot or on horse-

39

back, such as those of the Wallowas and the Blues, and
the pretty little lakes strung out along the Skyline Trail
of the Cascades. Other high lakes of the Oregon country
are large, well-known, and fairly heavily fished.

Among the well-known big lakes of the eastern high
country are Wallowa Lake near Joseph, and the Owyhee
Reservoir near Vale. In central Oregon there is a marvelous chain of big lakes just west of Bend along the shoulders of the Cascades. These include Hosmer Lake with
its landlocked Atlantic salmon, Odell, Crescent, and
Davis, as well as Crane Prairie and Wickiup Reservoirs
of the Deschutes River system, to name but a few.

A little further east, between Bend and Lapine, are
Paulina and East lakes. And to the north is Clear Lake,
headwaters for the McKenzie River. In south central
Oregon one finds Diamond Lake and Klamath Lake,
close to the California Line.

These are some of the best known fishing lakes in
the state. When I say they are heavily fished, I mean
that on weekends and major holidays during the mid-
summer season, you may encounter numbers of anglers.
Then again, on weekdays and during off-seasons you
may find but few or none.

Although unusually dry winters may put Cascade
streams and their lakes in readiness when the trout
season opens in late April, this is not usually the case.
As a rule I don't head for the high country until the last
days of May, for I have found woods roads blocked with
snow in places even this late in the year at altitudes
approaching six-thousand feet above sea level.

Looking at a detailed map of Oregon you'll notice a
chain of lakes grouped closely together just off Century
Drive west of Bend. These are Todd, Sparks, Elk, Little
and Big Lava, Little and Big Cultus, Devil's Lake, Crane
Prairie, North and South Twin, Wickiup, Davis, Waldo,
and Hosmer.

If you want to be awed by some of the most magnificent scenery in the nation, visit these waters in June. Century Drive (highway 46) will either take you directly there, or lead you to connecting forest roads. These woods roads are astonishingly good. You'll strike stretches where you'll need to drive carefully, but the average forest trace in this area, though it appears to have been made by a single swipe of a bulldozer blade, runs firmly over volcanic sand coated with pine needles.

This is a land of awesome stillness. Columns of forest giants line each trace, and the scene is one of serene yet wild beauty. Snowbanks may still lie in the heavy shade of June, warning travelers that this is indeed high country. Never try to negotiate these routes before mid-May, and even then consult the local forest service or the nearest general store.

My wife and I, sometimes accompanied by fishing friends, started visiting the high lakes of central Oregon many years ago. In those days we employed full tenting equipment, but in recent years we have used a small house trailer.

These lakes are best fished by boat. Some have boat rental facilities, but we always brought our own. For complete information about facilities at the lakes, consult the Oregon Department of Fish and Wildlife, the National Forest Service, or the State Highway Department. Most of the big lakes have forest camps on their shores, with picnic tables, water pumps, and outhouses.

Although wind directions may change should a storm pick up, the prevailing wind here in fair weather is from the west and northwest. Consequently it is a good idea to pitch your camp on a west or northwest shore. In this way you have fairly calm water near camp even on windy days.

A word of warning is needed here regarding the use of boats on these high lakes, some of which can kick up rough waves quite suddenly. Boats should never be overloaded and should be capable of riding out the tricky seas formed by close running white-caps.

The high lakes are usually placid in early morning and late evening, the best times to fish anyway, so time your across-the-lake expeditions to these hours, unless your boat can take anything the lake may offer when whipped by a stiff breeze. Crane Prairie, Wickiup, Waldo, Odell, Crescent, Diamond, Elk, Paulina, and even fairly small Thompson Reservoir can kick up wicked waves in a high desert wind.

Two other very good fishing lakes in the Prineville region that can kick up a heavy chop are Ochoco and Prineville reservoirs. Billy Chinook Lake, better known as Round Butte Reservoir, (which covers 2,500 acres and backs up the flow of the Deschutes, Metolius, and Crooked rivers) and Pelton Reservoir (which backs up eight miles of the Deschutes river below the Round Butte impoundment.) are also a far cry from farmland ponds, and the wise angler with tiny cartop boat should beware of wind and waves.

The boat I habitually use up here is a twelve-foot, fairly wide beamed Aluma-Craft, an aluminum boat of almost canoe shape which can take quite a bit of rough water with proper handling. Still I always keep a wary eye cocked to the weather. If, as occasionally happens, I see black thunderheads and rolling clouds approaching, I either make a quick run to camp or head for a sheltered shore.

On one occasion on Crane Prairie, when my wife and I were fishing with another couple in separate boats, we noticed dark clouds piling up in the southwest, shot through with lightning and rumbling ominously. A white sheet which seemed to hang below these clouds indicated hail.

We could have started for camp at once, and would have, except for the fact that our two fishing companions were using a very light, low-sided craft, and were tied to a log at the end of a long narrow arm of the big lake which was open to the sweep of the threatening storm. When they showed no indication of heading in, we opened our motor wide, intending to warn them of the impending danger. We were within a hundred yards of them when the storm struck.

I have been caught out on big water, in small craft, in quite a few storms in my time, but nothing in my experience can hold a candle to what happened that day. The wind came with hurricane force, driving before it a torrent of hailstones, some of which were as large as quarters. Waves whipping down the long narrow channel beat on the low sides of our friends' little dory, breaking over the gunwales. Hailstones battered my ears with a force that flapped them about and stung like fire. We took the woman aboard to lighten the tiny craft and, by taking it slowly, came safely to camp.

This storm came up suddenly on a beautiful sunny June day, and was just as suddenly gone. Within an hour the sun shone again, melting the three inches of hailstones that had accumulated in the bottom of the boat within the course of a few minutes. It was a thrilling experience, a never to be forgotten adventure for our rocking chair days. But in those few minutes, an unwary angler might have been swamped.

My one regret about this Crane Prairie experience is that I didn't break out a camera and photograph the surface of the lake under the lash of the storm. Those big hailstones made it appear as though the lake was under fire from a thousand heavy machine guns. Water spouted high in millions of jets as the stones struck, producing a scene of awesome beauty.

The same couple who were with us on Crane Prairie that day startled other anglers on another occasion by staying out in that same forty-five pound craft during a stiff blow that brought whitecaps to Wickiup Reservoir. Noticing folks on shore with binoculars trained on them,

I motored out to our friends, only to find them calmly reading magazines, rods hanging over the gunwale. This couple stoutly maintains that their tiny craft will take anything the high lakes can hand out. Don't you believe it. However, the average cartop boat is safe enough here if used with good judgment and a wary eye to wind and weather.

As much as we have traveled this high lake country, my wife and I would be hard pressed to select a favorite lake from the group. For numbers and variety of fish taken, Crane Prairie tops our list. We've had fishing on Crane Prairie that must be seen to be believed. Although Crane has never disappointed us on any of our trips, it served us best on a three-day trip in June.

On this expedition we came in by way of Davis Lake, hitting an arm of Wickiup first. We camped on Wickiup that night but did not launch our boat, content to take enough small rainbow from shore for the evening frying pan. As dusk came down we regretted that we hadn't launched. Trout began jumping all over the place, making rings and landing splashes in the water offshore that were large enough for salmon.

When those whoppers began their performance our camp came apart at the seams. We, too, began leaping about, putting rods together, tying on flies, pulling up our boots, rushing out into the lake as far as we could wade to make strenuous casts. Those rises were too far out for wading, but we tried. Alas, we didn't hook a single fish which, we agreed, must have been the big German browns for which Wickiup is famous.

Since our objective of the trip was Crane Prairie, we pulled out the next morning, driving some six miles on to the Quinn River camp on the lake. Quinn River camp is a delightful spot. Here the Quinn gushes from the side of the mountain fully born, with enough volume to float a boat the hundred or so yards down to the lake. The

Gray tied down wings

orange Palmer body

light brown throat hackle
size 4·6·8 on full sinking line

Ghostly grey spires thrust through the surface of Crane Prairie.

water issuing from the ground is ice cold and pure enough to drink. Camped beside this musical stream among widely separated ponderosa pines, we were just about as near to Paradise as it is possible to get on this earth.

Crane Prairie is not always clear in June. As is characteristic of most lakes, it may produce an algae bloom about this time of year. But on this occasion the lake was clear. We launched the boat, spent an hour preparing and eating lunch, then returned to the boat to find a school of good-sized rainbow enjoying its shade. This sort of thing really makes a fishing person sit up and take notice. Our nerves were vibrating like tuning forks as we proceeded below the fishing deadline (a marker hung on a tree) and motored out into the lake.

When Crane Prairie is clear it is an astonishing body of water. It is actually a reservoir, created many years ago when a dam was built across the Deschutes River. Before that, the Deschutes and Quinn rivers, Cultus Creek, and other creeks tributary to the Deschutes had wound across this terrain, forming a meadowland among heavy forest. The area was flooded with the forest left standing. Now deadened by water, the trees form a maze of ghostly grey spires that thrust through the surface of Crane Prairie, with channels winding among them. In areas that were former creek beds or meadowlands, we looked down to see the well-preserved skeletons of chaparral interwoven with avenues of white sand.

We anchored where we could cast down one of those avenues, rigging our fly rods with free-line reels strung with two-pound monofilament, clamping a single split shot two feet above a number eight hook. We baited with worms.

Casting into crystal-clear water, we watched the tiny split shot slowly pull our worms down. No trout were in sight. And then, as though materializing in place, there were trout striking at the bait. We wrist snapped the hooks home and were into the play with husky rainbows and eastern brook trout.

This was especially exciting for me, since it was the first time I had encountered really large eastern brooks since I fished as a lad in Massachusetts. We took only enough fish for camp meat, trout long enough to more than cover a good-sized frying pan, then returned to camp.

The next day we set out, determined to find the entrance to Cultus Arm, a long indentation we had heard about, that was created where Cultus River drained in from Cultus Lake. This turned out to be no simple chore. We cruised among thousands of dead timber spires, considerably confused until we finally found it, a long narrow canal of water which seemed but another lead into a timber maze, but which actually extends a mile or more before being blocked by fallen trees. Here we anchored and got into even more fantastic fishing.

We took rainbow to twenty-four inches, eastern brook to eighteen inches, fat scrappy fish, beautifully marked. We cast out, watching the point where the line entered the water as the lure slowly sank toward the bottom. When the line shot away we struck, usually hooking a trout. To make the sport even more interesting, we flattened the barbs of our hooks, changing from bait to streamer flies. We let the flies sink a few feet, then twitched them to give them action. I doubt if Alaska could produce faster trouting than this.

The next day, hoping to take pictures of this fabulous fishing, we coaxed four chance-met anglers to accompany us up Cultus Arm. We anchored them in the right place, then anchored ourselves a way off, breaking out our cameras. We were astonished when our fishermen could not hook into a fish. Since we had lured these fellows away from their trolling with wide-eyed tales of how hot the fishing was in the arm, we felt like a couple of dunces. Disgusted, the foursome left. We moved over to their anchorage and began casting to our hot spot.

Before the anglers were out of sight we had two leaping rainbows doing somersaults. Looking back they saw what was going on but continued on their way. That evening in camp we discussed this with them. The mystery was solved when we discovered that they had been using the same leaders on our crystal clear Cultus Arm water that they used in fall and winter on the coast for steelhead and salmon—fifteen pound monofilament. These men were veteran anglers on other waters, but they didn't have the slightest idea of how to fish the high lakes. Trolling with spinners held down with heavy sinkers, baited and otherwise, seems to be the method favored by the average Oregon angler. But we feel that this is the poorest possible way to fish either for creel or sport.

Ever since I was tall enough to sneeze without stirring up dust, I have been told that the colder the water (the nearer to ice) the livelier the trout. This simply isn't so. Trout are at their best, which is to say most hungry, when in water of their optimum temperature. For most species, this lies between 55 and 65 degrees. In water colder than this trout are not very active. The minnow eaten yesterday or last week, still lies half digested in the fish's stomach. Consequently trout are not inclined to chase a fast-moving lure trolled by a boat, usually at the wrong water depth for the temperature of the lake at the moment.

Trollers generally ply the water fairly close to the surface, although they think they are trolling deeper. If they happen to troll at the depth the fish like at the moment, slow enough for ice-cold fish to chase the lure down, they have good luck. If not, they go in with an empty creel. All lakes have various bands of temperature. In June, with feeder streams running through

48

snowbanks and nights getting down to frost, these high lakes are coldest at the surface and on the bottom. The trout select an in-between depth most suited to them.

Looking down into the clear water of Cultus Arm, I saw a school of rainbow lying at about the six-foot depth. Three feet or more below them were the eastern brook. I believe the sockeye salmon were even deeper. These bands of temperature vary throughout the lake, affected by such things as wave action and other factors. We recommend a fishing method that allows you to fish at all depths with every cast.

These high lakes are ideal for light gear. The fly rod equipped with a shooting head line for long casts, or the spinning rod with hardware or bait are best. We use only fly rods here, but alternate between fly reels and lines when fishing with flies, and free-line casting reels strung with light monofilament when using bait. With this sort of rig one can cover a lot of water around an anchored boat, and with a drifting boat, one can work a wide swath across the lake.

With every cast, using a single tiny split shot for sinker weight, sometimes with none, our lures sink slowly through all depths of water. With every foot or two of sink we twitch the rod tip to give the lure action and attract the trout's attention. This method really works, no matter at what depth the fish lie.

Later in the year, when trout are more active in warmer water, trolling will produce better than in June. But still, the fight of the fish is held down with hardware and heavy sinkers. If you like to cast, and to take large trout on light tackle, give our method a try. It requires no particular skill on the part of the angler, except a bit of deft handling in the play on two-pound leader.

On Crane Prairie in June I once sank the barb into a rainbow that had me wishing my leader had more breaking strength. My wife and I were letting the boat drift with the breeze, casting here and there, when this fish struck. It fought like a steelhead, but it seemed I could handle it on the light tackle. Since we were drifting into snags, I yelled for Laurel to heave out the anchor. Heave she did, with a resulting splash that drenched us both and spooked my fish.

When that rainbow jumped and I saw the broad beam of its body, I almost had heart failure. This was the kind of rainbow one dreams of. I finally scooped it up in the net, but it was so heavy that it went right through the bottom of the mesh, and I found myself playing the monster through the hole in the net!

There was more yelling and excitement around there than if we'd had a wildcat climb aboard. By the time I was able to gill the fish and hoist it in, I was really wrung out. This rainbow was not much longer than others I had taken on Crane Prairie, but it was much heavier through the shoulders, the largest rainbow I have ever taken from Oregon's high lakes.

As the days warm, the trout of these lakes begin to take dry flies at dusk. We carry a compact fly-tying kit along and tie what flies we require. On Crane Prairie I prefer black gnats, red ants, dusky millers, mosquitos and blue uprights. The light and dark Cahill flies are good bets since they imitate many kinds of Mayflies. Use size ten. For wet fly-fishing, any size six fly that imitates a swimming minnow, with a white deer hair or marabou wing, is good. On Wickiup, where there are large browns, I tie a special fly on a number four long-shanked hook. It has an orange, Palmer tied body with light brown throat hackle and a gray bucktail wing, tied down.

Tying your own flies is an interesting facet of the fishing game. We like to believe that flies we tie will produce better than standard models, but doubt that this is often the case. The smart angler, however, does ask the veteran what he is using, and listens closely to the reply.

No trout that swims these waters puts up the fight that is handed out by the landlocked sockeye, the kokanee or blueback, which are found in Crane Prairie, Big Cultus, Odell, Crescent, Elk, and possibly in other lakes in this area. This fish is easily identified by its silver body, having no black spots, and with a narrowing before the tail common to all salmon. The kokanee has red meat that provides better eating than any trout found here, except possibly the brookie.

Since kokanee tend to school, you may fish the lake rather thoroughly without contacting them. On Crane Prairie we found kokanee at the mouth of the Quinn River and at the mouth of Cultus Arm. When hooked, they tend to go into a series of bewildering acrobatics. Once you find them, you can usually count on some good entertainment and a real fast time.

Kokanee are often taken on troll, but we prefer to use nightcrawlers, putting the bait on the bottom with a buckshot, then slowly moving it about. Actually, the first one we took on Crane Prairie hit a worm held up by a cork bobber, which I had tossed out as we idled while eating lunch.

These high lakes can keep an angler busy for a life-time, and even then one would not have time to sample more than a small percentage of their possibilities. There's Odell, Crescent, and Big Cultus, famed for mackinaw. There's Wickiup, with its large browns mingling with eastern brook, rainbow, Dolly Varden, and kokanee.

Crescent is also noted for kokanee. Crane Prairie offers its vast numbers of rainbow. Davis Lake challenges the angler with big rainbow on a fly. Big Lava gives up good catches of brook trout, and Diamond Lake produces big rainbow and Kamloops trout. East and Paulina lakes are popular for rainbow, brook, and some large brown trout. North and South Twin lakes offer rainbow. There's crystalline Waldo Lake, (largest of the group and seldom reachable by road before late June), and Elk Lake, a beautiful body of water right on paved Century Drive which contains brook, rainbow, and kokanee. And Sparks. And Todd. And Little Cultus. I mention Little Cultus last of this group because I think this small, amethyst water deserves special consideration.

My wife and I had been camped at Quinn River on Crane Prairie for several days when we decided to move camp to the headwaters of the Deschutes, Cow Camp at the north end of Crane. That put us only two miles from Little Cultus Lake. In spite of the prime angling that we were enjoying on the Deschutes, we decided to haul our aluminum boat to Little Cultus for a day.

With a savory lunch packed, the boat slung atop our car, and the outboard motor in the rear deck, we pulled a mile off Century Drive to reach Little Cultus. Covering about two acres, this lake is a real jewel, deep blue at its center, shading to light green near some of its more shallow shores. We found the lake to be deserted. No boat but ours moved over its surface.

There is a challenge in tackling a new and unknown water, and an eagerness to explore the secrets it may hold. Little Cultus seemed, during our first hour of fishing, to hold nothing more interesting than six to eight-inch rainbow and brook trout. We motored about its shores, casting flies. Then we tried the cold, blue depths, using worms. In exasperation I began trolling various spoons and plugs, then attached my most deadly trout lure, the double-bladed Indiana spinner in size six, brass and nickle finish, trailed by a night crawler strung on a number eight hook.

Though this rig did not produce any trout, I noticed that when we made a turn, so that the lure slowed and sank deeper than when we were under way in a straight line, I got a few very light pecking strikes. I felt that these strikes were from small trout like the ones we had taken with flies along the shore, but as time went on I began to develop a sneaking hunch that such might not be the case.

Analyzing the situation, it seemed that there must be large trout present in these deep waters, and since they had not taken deeply sunken bait, they might be off their feed at the moment, though aroused enough to peck halfheartedly at the whirling spinner blades. I reasoned that a slowly moving spinner close to the bottom might attract them. Once attracted, a slowly moving bait right on the bottom might take them. To bring this about we dropped anchor and began casting our baited spinners as far as we could.

We let them sink all the way to the bottom, then reeled them very slowly, practically crawling the spinner on the bottom. I got a series of the same light pecking strikes that I had experienced on the trolling turn. Instantly I dropped the lure and let it lie motionless. Then I picked it up, reeling rapidly. The strike was solid and sure; a fourteen-inch eastern brook arched into the air in a three-foot leap. This solved the problem for that particular day on Little Cultus. The trout were beautifully marked, with gorgeous color and delicious flavor.

One of my favorite eastern Oregon lakes is Thompson Reservoir, about sixteen miles out of Silver Lake on a red-rocked forest road off Highway 31. Every year I journey here in late May or early June with an Aloha caravan, made up of sportsmen who own Aloha vacation trailers and campers. A few picnic tables, an iron pump delivering ice-cold water, and a couple of Chick Sales toilets are the only conveniences found at the campgrounds. But the fishing is fabulous for Kamloops trout, a cousin of the rainbow which run ten to twenty-four inches. At this time of year these fish provide excellent eating, though later in the year they develop a muddy taste. They hit best on either trolled or cast silver flatfish in the smaller sizes, or on deftly handled flies.

The on-the-road lakes of the Cascades are for those who like to take along camping gear in the family car or use trailers or pickup campers. For hardier souls there are scores, hundreds of mountain lakes which can be reached by well-marked hiking trails. And then there are other lakes, their numbers legion, which separate the men from the boys. These are but pinpoints on detailed forest maps, gems of blue water unmarked by trail. Many have been planted by airplane. Let's touch on these hidden bodies of water.

THE OFF-ROAD LAKES

ALTHOUGH THE OREGON COUNTRY IS WORLD FAMOUS for its numerous fishing streams, it is not generally thought of as a land of many lakes. This is unjustified. In addition to lakes that can be reached by car, discussed in the previous chapter, there are almost a thousand lakes approachable only on foot or horseback in the Cascade and Wallowa mountains alone.

What is even more intriguing to the angling enthusiast is the fact that some three hundred of these off-road lakes are stocked with rainbow and eastern brook trout, the easiest to reach stocked annually, the more remote every two or three years. Imagine blazing a trail through primeval timber, emerging at last at the blue waters of an unknown lake. It is a mental picture to fire the imagination of the adventurous angler.

In the primal stillness of the forest, an angler savors a keen sense of exhilaration, a oneness with the frontiersman of an earlier day who may have passed this way when America was young. What's more, the fellow gets fish! These hidden lakes are so plentiful that many have yet to be named, or fished, although many have been planted with trout by air.

The largest clusters of off-road lakes fall within seven areas. They are Olallie Lakes and Mt. Jefferson, Marion Lake Basin, Mink Lakes, Taylor Burn, Sky Lakes, Mountain Lakes, and Wallowa Wilderness. For detailed road and trail information, see the U.S. Forest Service maps for Mt. Hood, Willamette, Rogue River, Winema, and Wallowa-Whitman National Forests. Wilderness maps published by the Forest Service offer a close-up of each of the lake areas contained within wilderness boundaries, including topographic detail. Topographic information for other lake areas is available on the U.S. Geological Survey sectional maps of Oregon.

There are approximately twenty-six lakes in the Olallie group, ranging in size from sixty acre Lower Lake to one acre Sheep Lake. The basin is within the boundaries of Mt. Hood National Forest and is the closest group to Portland, Oregon's largest city. The roads in the area and the major hiking trails are both fairly well maintained by the U.S. Forest Service. There are ranger stations at the north end of Olallie Lake and at Breitenbush Lake.

The Pacific Crest Trail leads directly from Breitenbush Lake to Jefferson Park, in the northern part of the Mt. Jefferson Wilderness, Willamette National Forest. Jefferson Park is an alpine meadow at the northern base of Mt. Jefferson, containing a sprinkling of small deep lakes in one of the prettiest settings anywhere in Oregon. The mountain towers above the basin, with its giant boulders, blue glaciers, and ever-changing cloud patterns. By mid-summer the meadow is carpeted with wild flowers, and Bays Lake and Scout offer good fishing for brook trout.

Pamelia Lake, also in the Mt. Jefferson Wilderness on the mountain's southwest flank, is a short easy hike for small but plentiful brook trout, and Hunts Cove, with its twin lakes Hunts and Hanks a short steep hike beyond Pamelia, offers cutthroat and rainbow fishing in a picturesque setting.

The Marion Lake group is in the southern part of the Mt. Jefferson Wilderness, Willamette National Forest, east of Salem and Corvallis. Three Fingered Jack is the nearest glacial peak. Marion Lake itself is one of the largest lakes in Oregon that cannot be reached by car. It contains rainbow and cutthroat trout. There are thirty-four lakes in the Marion basin known to be worth fishing, ranging in size from 353 acre Marion down to one acre Alice, North, and South. There are four geographically distinct lake groups in the basin, identified as Marion, Duffy, Scar Mountain, and Square. Most of these waters have been stocked with eastern brook trout. Trails are usually passable by the latter part of June.

The Mink Lake basin is within the Three Sisters Wilderness area of the Willamette and Deschutes National Forests west of Bend and east of Eugene. The basin includes thirty-one lakes known to contain fish, and many others that might be worth an angler's attention. Geography and connecting trails tend to cluster the lakes into the Lucky Lake group, Horse Lake group, Mink Lake group, and Sister Mirror group. Mink Lake is the largest of the basin, covering 300 acres. Most of these lakes are adjacent to the famous Pacific Crest Trail, which runs unbroken from Mexico to Canada.

The Taylor Burn area, just south of the Three Sisters Wilderness in the Willamette and Deschutes National forests, contain roughly forty fishing lakes ranging in size from five hundred acre Charlton (less than a mile off the road) down to three acre Emma, with several lakes in the group topping fifty acres or more. Rainbow trout predominate here, but there is a goodly sprinkling of eastern brook.

There's a forest camp high up at Irish and Taylor lakes, which may be reached by a very primitive road (usually open for travel in July). From there one can step onto the Pacific Crest Trail heading north toward the largest cluster of lakes in this group. Trailheads to other lakes in the area are located at north Waldo Lake, Skookum Creek, and the Taylor Burn Guard Station, to name but a few of many access points.

The Sky Lakes Wilderness includes four separate lake basins within the Rogue River and Winema National Forests just south of Crater Lake National Park and west of Klamath Lake. From north to south they are Seven Lakes, Sky Lakes, McKee (formerly Dwarf Lakes), and Blue Canyon. These are the headwaters of Oregon's famous Rogue River.

There are at least nineteen lakes here especially worth an angler's attention, ranging from ninety-acre Heavenly Twins down to five acre Donna and Pear, and many more worth a day's exploring. Most of these waters contain eastern brook, but some are also stocked with rainbow. This is rugged country, but there are established camps at many of the lakes, and most of the trails are well enough maintained, with the Pacific Crest Trail winding right through the heart of the Wilderness.

Seven Lakes Basin, the northernmost lake group, is just off the Pacific Crest Trail, reached by track from Sevenmile Marsh forest camp, or by a longer route from Sky Lakes and Dwarf Lakes trailheads to the south. Grass Lake offers the best fishing of this group for eastern brook trout up to 18 inches. These brookies are especially fat and succulent, with pink and red striped meat.

Other good lakes in the vicinity include Cliff, Middle, and Alta, one of the last lakes up here to thaw.

Sky Lakes and McKee basins are best reached by trail from Cold Springs forest camp. Isherwood and the Heavenly Twins, in the McKee group, offer good fishing for eastern brook and rainbow. Natasha and Elizabeth are also worth exploring. Marguerette and Horseshoe of the Sky Lakes group are stocked with both brook and rainbow and are good bets in early and late summer.

Blue Canyon Basin is accessible by some strenuous hiking from the McKee Basin, and from trail heads near Big Meadows on the east side of the basin or Saddle camp on the west. A trail from Upper South Fork in the Winema Forest actually follows a fork of the Rogue River right up to this group of six or seven good trout lakes and other intriguing ponds. A shorter trail heads in from Blue Rock.

The Mountain Lakes Wilderness is within the Winema National Forest just a short drive from Klamath Falls, Fort Klamath, Medford, and Ashland. It contains seven major lakes, ranging in size from 70 acre Harriette down to three acre Meb and Zeb. Brook trout are the main species here, with some rainbow at Harriette and Como. Echo, Clover, and South Pass are all worth exploring. This is rugged country, rocky peaks interwoven with lush meadow, and usually not open till the end of June. I personally prefer to come here in August. By September one already needs to be on the lookout for early snows.

Last but not least are the lakes of the Wallowa Mountains in Wallowa-Whitman National Forest. This is generally considered to be packtrain country, though the angler with a good pair of legs and lungs, a sleeping bag, and grub sack can really have a time high in this wild blue yonder. There are about twenty-eight lakes that offer good trout fishing, ranging in size from ninety acre Long down to two acre Echo. Eastern brooks are the main species here, and they are numerous.

No roads cross the Wallowa mountains or access any of its lakes other than big Wallowa Lake itself. The entire mountain range, with its rugged peaks, sparkling brooks, and hidden lakes is contained within the boundaries of the Eagle Cap Wilderness. You can enter the area from the north by way of roads out of the towns of Minam, Wallowa, Lostine, Enterprise, and Joseph. Jump-off points in the south are Medical Springs, Baker, or Halfway. In the west, roads lead into the mountains from Union and Cove. Packers are available at many points.

You can take a crack at these lakes as early as June, but July or even August are much preferred. Many of these lakes are big enough to be frustrating to an angler standing on shore. When fish begin rising in the evening beyond casting distance, one is inclined to jump in and swim out there. This water is really cold! A rubber raft would be ideal to have along, but even the smallest size is really too bulky if you're on foot in this steep terrain. I prefer to carry everything I need to build a raft, including a sharp three-quarter ax, spikes, and rope.

In addition to these large lake areas, there are many lakes scattered singly or in smaller groupings throughout the mountains of the Oregon Country, particularly in the Cascades. A good number of these are still unnamed, and trails to them have yet to be blazed, but they have often been planted with trout by air. What a windfall awaits the angler spunky enough to seek them out. Many other lakes are approached by good trails. There are at least thirty-five such lakes in the central Oregon Cascades in the region of Summit Lake west of Odell Lake, in and around the Diamond Peak Wilderness. Suzanne and Darlene in the Deschutes National Forest, and Indigo in the Umpqua Forest are worth a crack.

Not far off Willamette Pass Highway are the three Rosary lakes, and Upper and lower Marilyn Lakes can

8' logs
8-spikes & 50' rope

mosquito

black Gnat

I carry everything I need to build a raft.

be approached by trail from the Gold Lake Road in this same area. Bobby Lake is one of the finest in the forest. A one mile hike from the Waldo Lake road, it covers forty acres and contains a mess of brook and rainbow trout.

Another lake pocket worth exploring is the Yoran Lake group, nestled under the northeast slope of Diamond Peak. The trail to these takes off from the west end of Odell. Along the McKenzie Pass, east of Eugene and west of the lava beds, are Frog, Scott, Linton, Benson, and Tenas, with good campgrounds at Frog and Scott.

Hiking into Oregon's high off-road lakes requires some forethought. Can the trip be made in one day, allowing time for the fishing? Does someone else know where you are going so that, should you run into trouble, your absence will be noted and rescue made possible? If the trip cannot be made in one day, are you equipped, with both gear and woods savvy, for an overnight stay? Do you have what you need for an uneventful trip as well and an ordinary emergency? Do have the right tackle? Or too much? Is every item in your pack really necessary?

I recall a time when I hiked into back country, seeking a lake which was rumored to lie nestled beneath the snowy crown of Mount Tallac in the California Sierras, south of Lake Tahoe in the wild Hell's Hole area. I carried equipment on that trip that I didn't need, and generally lacked what was required. Consequently, a fine Heddon casting rod and reel lie somewhere beside an outlet of that lake, which I eventually found. Had I but consulted a Forest Service or other detailed map before starting out, I would have saved miles of rough country hiking and escaped a dangerous climb up a waterfall.

The searching for that lake took longer than I'd expected. I should have been equipped to stay overnight at 7000 feet altitude, but wasn't. Being considerable of a roughneck, I didn't need blankets or a sleeping bag as long as I had a hand ax, or at least a heavy knife to fashion a shelter and cut wood for a fire. But I didn't have these items, either.

What I did have was a large wicker fishing creel, absolutely useless for a such a trip, since strenuous hiking usually churns up any cached trout into a mass of bones and mush. Furthermore, when I was clinging to the side of that cliff beneath the waterfall, that darned creel nearly got me flung off into space when it swung around beneath my belly. I had also brought in two rods, in order to handle any kind of fishing the trip might offer. I lost one in the shuffle.

I had a whale of a time looking for that hidden lake. The years have softened memories of the annoyances and put a shine to the pleasures, and in the balance I look back on the trip as one of the best. Yet, when I hunkered down that night with a chill wind on my spine and my toes curled in shrunken canvas shoes, the situation looked mighty grim.

Today, by the way, I use a five-ounce, eight-foot fly rod and carry along two reels. One reel is filled with forward shooting head fly line, the other, a free-line gadget, is loaded with a hundred yards of light monofilament. This outfit casts just about as efficiently as regular spinning gear.

One comforting thought about these isolated and roadless lakes is that, should the day ever come when our big lakes are fished out, these hidden waters will still be there and in their prime.

Late June, July, and August are the months to hit the high off-road lakes of the Oregon country, though in some years they may be good into September, and not snowed in even in October. I quite often fish some of the high lakes in October when I am in eastern Oregon on the annual deer hunt, but I seldom touch these waters in August and September.

When August comes, my thoughts turn to the streams of the Oregon coast. I exchange the sweet scent of high country pine for the pungency of the sea, for fog streamers drifting in through the passes of the Coast Range at dawn. I'm drawn there like steel to the magnet, particularly if there has been a rain. Out in the sea the gorgeous sea-run cutthroat, sometimes called harvest trout, and their acrobatic companions the chinook and silver jack salmon, are moving into the tide-water sections of coastal streams.

Ah, me, this is the stuff that make up fishermen's dreams: tawny tideland meadows along the Salmon and the Siletz, the Alsea and the Nestucca, the Wilson and the Trask; sea gulls wheeling in air scented with salt and kelp and fir forest, with a low tide at dawn when jacks leap in the eddies. Let's take a look at the coast in August.

THE COAST IN AUGUST

IN EARLY AUGUST THE COASTAL STREAMS are low and clear, running musically over stony riffles from the summit of the Coast Range to the sea. Fishing here now is apt to bring about a slaughter of the innocents unless care is used, for the pools are alive with three to six-inch fingerling steelhead and salmon. Such fish cannot be legally creeled on the coast streams, where an eight-inch length minimum is in force.

It is beautiful on the coast at this time of year. Vine maple are touched with crimson, and the alders are yellowing to gold, even though there has been no frost. For those who live here, this is a time of expectancy. Folks move about with their eyes turned often to the sky, their weather senses alert for the first sign of a weather change that might indicate rain is on the way.

They know that when the first rainfall soughs in from the southwest on a warm wind, the great sea-run cutthroat trout will move in from the Pacific, scrappy and succulent.

When I arrive on the coast in August I perform a ritual which has been my secret for many years, and which discloses to me at once whether the sea-runs are in or not. I go to the upstream side of the bridge over the Salmon River at Rose Lodge. I lean far out over the east end of the bridge, peering down into the deep, clear water of the Bridge Pool. Beneath me I see a ledge of rock running parallel to the river, perhaps six feet beneath the surface. In this rock, so deep down that you must shade your eyes to see it, there is a U-shaped indentation which is about two feet wide and two feet deep. If the sea-run cutts are in, one or more of them will be lying in this indentation.

If they are not there, I know that I have a few more days to wait. If they are there, my fisherman's heart beats a bit faster, for I know that the fabulous days of fall coastal fishing have started and that there will be a grand time here until the coastal season closes in March.There are many places where one can peer down into coastal rivers to ascertain whether the sea-run cutts are in, but my spot on the Salmon River has never given me a false report.

Just because the sea-runs are in does not necessarily mean that fishermen not well acquainted with them will put cutts in the creel. The anglers who have been skunked on early run cutts are legion. There will be times later in the year when these gorgeous trout can be quite easily taken from coastal streams. But in August, with the water low and clear after the first spattering of rain, only those who know their habits and inclinations will be able to feast on the tastiest trout of all. I know this from experience, for no man has taken a worse beating from these trout than I over a period of years.

I recall when I lived on the Salmon River, a stone's throw from the Rose Lodge bridge. I was in a position to fish for them every day, and the early run cutts exasperated me no end. Marion Huffman, Rose Lodge tackle dealer and expert coastal fisherman, worked with me that August to defeat these wary fish.

Peering down into the water from the bridge we could see beauties up to two feet long, lying motionless in the depths. We hastened to fetch our rods and tried everything in the book. We went down to the river in the morning, and we fished in midday and toward evening without result. We used wet and dry flies, angleworms, spinners, plugs, and spoons. We chased crawdads and used their tails. The more we failed, the more we determined to succeed.

Finally, we decided to look up the time of sunrise and sunset, and to try fishing the first legal minute in the morning and the last legal minute at night.

The river ran dark and mysterious the next morning when we arrived at the Rose Lodge pool. It was so dark at the first minute of legal fishing, an hour before sunrise, that we had to use a flashlight to bait our hooks with wiggling worms. Standing above the bridge, I made my first cast. I couldn't see where the cast landed or where the line drifted. As we fished we talked in whispers, not knowing why, only that whispers seemed fitting.

Suddenly the surface of the pool exploded with a leaping fish. It jumped all over the place. We watched it for several moments before I realized it was jumping on my loose line. I got into the play then, landing the first sea-run cutthroat of the season. It was eighteen inches long, as broad as the palm of my hand, fat as butter. We took seven more that morning, one of which measured twenty-two inches.

This fishing experience took place many years ago, and it taught me something about sea-run cutts that I didn't know before. This has stood me in good stead upon many occasions since. Last fall I stopped at the Rose Lodge bridge in August and joined a group of very discouraged fishermen. I listened to their tales of woe, and gazed down into the water where they pointed. Gorgeous sea-run cutthroat trout were hanging in the clear water, motionless save for the opening and closing of their gills.

"Nobody can catch those beauties," I was told. "Believe us, we know. We've been trying to catch them all week without a strike. Man, we've used everything on them that we can dream up."

I parked my car beneath the trees. I watched the sun sink below firs that tower above the canyon. The stillness of dusk slid down upon the water. I knew that now was the time, and that if I hurried down to the river's edge I would have an hour to fish—an hour which might be very interesting, for fish which supposedly couldn't be caught.

Since this was evening, not morning, and we'll have a word about this later, I moved below the bridge, instead of above as Marion Huffman had done at dawn. I strung a number eight bucktail caddis on a nine-foot leader tapered to two-pound breaking strength, then slipped silently up to where the water in the pool broke over into the rapid at the tailings. I cast the fly high, letting it drift slowly and deeply, straining my eyes to watch the line where it entered the water. When it began to shoot away, I set the hook and was into a trout that came out of the drink in leaps of liquid silver. I lost this one in a flurry of acrobatics, but took two before legal fishing time elapsed.

In sea-runs we have a fish that spends half of its time in fresh water and half of it in salt. When carrying its sea colors of pure silver, it is a different fish than when it turns back to stream coloration, with a dark green back, silver sides dotted black, fins and throat

Suddenly the surface of the water exploded.

slashed deep red. The stream cutthroat is a fast water fish, loving the current. The newly arrived sea-run is accustomed to the calm depths of the ocean where it is hidden from prying eyes. It prefers to lie in deep slow moving pools during the hours of daylight. Lying there immobile all day, it awaits darkness before venturing in search of food in the clear water of August.

When dusk comes down, or during the darkness before dawn, it cruises about eagerly, seeking crawdads and other bottom food, rising to take surface tidbits as they become available. These stretches when feeding time and legal angling overlap are brief, so make the most of them.

You'll find most of your feeding sea-runs in the lower portions of the pool where the gravel shelves up to the rapid, providing an ideal place for crawdads to linger and for pool flotsam to settle. These trout are migrating upstream. In August their milt and roe sacks are not yet bulging, so their urgency for the upstream spawning beds is not yet strong upon them. They do have a tendency to move upstream at dusk, and an occasional fish can be taken at the entering rapid of the pool.

At dawn, entering rapids are often the very best places. The big trout have fed at night and tend to move up before daylight, if this is their inclination. They crowd toward the head of the pool, on the move, ready to hit. Keen competition at dusk may cause sea-runs to feed at the entering rapids, to beat the fish at the foot of the pool to the punch. Nevertheless, fully 75 percent of dusk-taken sea-runs will be taken at the foot of the pools, while the percentage will be just the opposite at dawn.

Native Oregonians' lack of zest for the fly in trouting has resulted in few sea-run cutts being taken on the feathers. This fish is one of the best fly fish in the state. Whenever I take a sea-run cutt on other than a fly, I always have a sneaking feeling that I am beating myself out of the best sport.

Occasionally, and when I do this it always surprises me, I have taken these harvest trout on dry flies during daylight hours, when the sun was on the water. This is the exception rather than the rule. If you are ever fortunate enough to hit these high-jumping acrobats on dry flies, you will enjoy an experience never to be forgotten.

I recall the fabulous trip I took with Don Mitchell, then chairman of the Oregon Game Commission, on the Siletz River in September. On that memorable occasion I swam the river after dark while wearing a four-hundred buck camera.

Don Mitchell is a large, good-humored man, and a very adept fisherman. We set out from his drugstore in Taft to drift the Siletz in a rubber raft from the Cedar Creek Hole to the Big Eddy. When we launched the raft above Don's summer cottage, where we left my wife and Don's dog, we could see the river's bottom clearly, regardless of water depth. I'd have sworn there wasn't a fish anywhere about.

We drifted halfway through a long, deep, and narrow pool. Don grasped the brush on shore to halt our drift. We sat waiting for the sun to sink below the rim of the canyon wall. The stillness was so intense that it buzzed in our ears like the inside of a conch shell.

Slowly the red ball of sun dipped below the forest on the ridgetop to the south and west. Dark shadows eased down the steep slopes to the pool's still surface. Suddenly to our right a fish rose, quietly and without commotion. Widening circles rippled across the water's surface. A man not in the know would have sworn that a fingerling had risen to take a midge. Yet this fish was eighteen inches long.

Mitchell rose to his knees in the wobbly rubber raft. He laid a red and white streamer exactly in the center of the rise. He let it lie there for a few moments, then twitched it. The results of the twitch were instantaneous. The bottom of the river blew up.

71

"Got him!" Mitchell grunted as he set the hook.

After this fish we drifted slowly. Rises came with regularity now. We cast to them, giving line to make up for the drift of the boat, letting the fly lie motionless for a moment, then bringing it to life with a movement of the rod tip. We drifted away from rises that left us hungering. We had no time to linger in one spot with darkness fast coming down.

On the outside curve of the Big Eddy, where shallow water and a clam bed lay against a plot of green meadow, we took enormous sea-run cutts, fish over twenty inches long and as broad as the palms of our hands. After ten fish, we called it a day, drifting on to where the river passed Don's cottage. This is where the exasperating dog greeted us.

You'd have to know this particular dog to know how it was. I maintain that the animal is nuts. Don swears that it is just a bit playful, and very loving.

When we hit the tailings of the Big Eddy we had to get out of the raft to float it through shallow water. Don dropped his fly box, containing some very special flies tied for him by Oregon's Frank Wire. In trying to retrieve the flies as they floated past me, I stepped into a hole, got dunked in the river, and had to swim out. Naturally, with boots and an expensive camera full of water, I was anxious to get ashore at the cabin, where Laurel waited with the dog.

This dog is a joyful creature, a very large wooly-coated individual, with eyes that grow sad or merry as the occasion demands. The dog feels that folks should be greeted enthusiastically when they arrive after even the shortest absence. Above all, he feels that any boat in which Don Mitchell rides should also have a spot for his wooly carcass.

We were floating down the river in total darkness now. Don was rowing frantically with the inadequate oars which are furnished with a two-man rubber raft, trying to make the shore before the fast current took us by the cabin landing. I was standing up in the raft, too wet to sit, holding the two rods and assorted gear, when we were assaulted by this gleeful hound. He came bounding down the steep way, leaped into the river, and swam toward the raft, yelping like a steam calliope.

Don was yelling for the dog to go away. My wife was screaming from shore. Heeding nothing, the wooly, yapping torpedo came on, boarding us with a splash that drenched everything within a twenty-foot radius. Don heroically rose to the occasion. He grasped the welcoming canine and tossed him back into the drink.

Unfortunately, he had both our flies stuck in his thick coat. Baying like a bear hound on trail, the dog swam 'round and 'round the raft. With each circle he unwound line from the two reels on the rods I held, wrapping us in line like trussed flounders.

Meanwhile, we were rapidly drifting by the cottage. Everyone, including the dog, was sounding off at peak volume. Finally, the hound dashed back to greet my wife. When he came to the ends of the lines, he spun me and the rubber raft like a top, almost tossing us into the drink. Fortunately the leaders were light enough to break off. We sat up half the night developing the film, and it cost me forty bucks to have the camera dried out and repaired. But the memory is priceless.

Early season angling for sea-runs starts in July on most coastal streams. It primarily involves trolling spinners and worms, or spinners and crawdad tails in the tidewater sections of these rivers. Clear water angling above salt usually starts in August after the first spatter of fall rains, with September the best month, particularly for the use of flies.

Once the heavy rains of October bring the river to flood, fly fishing for sea-runs gives way to bait or hardware. Fortunately for the survival of this marvelous sport fish, the heaviest runs come in when anglers are more interested in salmon than in trout. Also, a wise Department of Fish and Wildlife changed the trout opening on the coastal strip from April to late May. Some anglers won't agree with me that this was a wise move, but in my book it stopped the senseless slaughter of these fine fish when they were returning to sea from spawning, white-meated, lean and worthless in the frying pan.

There is a small upstream migration of prime summer sea-run cutts in some coastal rivers in May. Veteran anglers have long been aware of these fish, though they seldom are taken by the average fisherman. I took a real skunking from these May harvest trout in the company of an angler whom I consider to be the top fisherman of the nation, Ted Trueblood, former fishing editor of *Field and Stream*.

Ted had been in the habit of dropping in at my lodge on the Salmon River during the winter months to fish with me for steelhead trout. On this occasion he stopped by in May.

"Let's go fishing," he said as he poked his head through my doorway.

I hated to take him out at a time when I thought the river contained only three to five-inch steelhead and salmon fingerlings. Ted had never been on the Salmon River when it was at its summer low. Yet he instinctively selected a spot where some of these husky cutthroats lay. He took three while I was thoroughly skunked on my own river.

I returned to this particular riffle the next May, discovering that I had to use a long and very finely tapered leader with a dark, lightly dressed wet fly drifted deep and slow. These May fish hit so savagely that I broke off several on the strike. Once hooked, they are even more acrobatic than their autumn brothers. Do not confuse these fresh spring sea-run specimens with the lean and spawned-out cutthroat which are returning to sea after spawning in early spring.

After the heavy fall rains, if you don't become too salmon crazy to pay attention to trout, you will find the harvest trout quite easy to take. The water is high and roiled now, the migration is in full swing, and the harvest trout's early clear water caution has dimmed.

When rain is coming down in torrents and the water ouzels are singing their hearts out, you'll see big cutthroat arrowing up through the rapids, leaping here and there. Wendell Boyes, Newberg tackle dealer and expert angler, quite often lets the salmon go hang at such times. He fishes for these large trout with single salmon eggs drifted through the riffles, or casts small spoons and wobblers to get their attention.

One of the best baits I know for fall harvest trout is a chunk of white meat cut from the pestiferous mud-cats of the coastal rivers. This bait is legal in Oregon, though only on coastal streams. Artificials with crawdad colors produce well, too.

The sea-run cutthroat trout is one of the wonders of nature. It goes to sea with a green back and dark sides spotted black. There is a brilliant red band of color at the jaw line on each side, from which this fish derives its name. The flesh is almost colorless. Returning from the sea, the same trout is a symphony in silver, its red throat gash barely pink.

This fish has caused more arguments than any trout I know, even among veteran anglers who should know better. I quite frequently meet anglers who have fished the coastal streams for years, perhaps for a lifetime, who stoutly maintain that the sea-run cutthroat, known to them only as *harvest trout*, is not one and the same as the river cutthroat. I find myself pondering this stubborn attitude, in the face of the evidence at hand to the contrary. I have a sneaking hunch that many of these old-timers continue to deny that the cutthroat and harvest trout are one and the same from a reluctance to give up a myth of the past, as a child is reluctantly forced to give up belief in the existence of Santa Claus.

Down through the long years, from the days of Lewis and Clark, there has been this fish which appears at harvest time. The very name smacks of an October moon. Whether we call them cutthroat or harvest trout, sea-run are one of my favorite fish. But as much as I admire these scrappy, high-jumping beauties, my first love on the coast in early fall is the jack salmon. There is something about jack salmon fishing that gets under my hide. To meet them, let us move from the upstream rapids to the tidewaters of the Oregon coast.

SECRETS OF THE JACKS

FISHERMEN WHO KNOW THE SECRETS OF THE JACKS are fortunate indeed. Jack salmon are thick-bodied, very strong, very active juvenile salmon, all males. Their biting moods are strongly affected by wind, weather, and tides. Fishing for them requires a study of these natural phenomena, and is a sport different from any other in the Oregon country.

Jacks cannot be taken in passing by the casual angler. You can never take jack salmon by accident. You take them with studied intent.

One summer I was fishing for jacks with three companions at the Red Barn Hole of the Salmon River below Otis. A little way from our position another angler, a stranger to us, laced into a fish that ran off with a power drive, then came back fast, handing the fisherman an armful of loose line. Then it shot beneath his boat, breaking his rod tip off on the gunwale. The entire action, from hooking to broken rod, lasted only three or four seconds.

"That," the astonished angler declared, "was a chinook!"

At that moment there was a terrific eruption in the Red Barn Hole as a giant chinook hen, already dark from tidewater, leaped and crashed into the drink with a sound like a cow falling from a cutbank.

"You're wrong, my friend," Marion Huffman said. "*That* was a chinook. All you had on was a jack. They're small, but rough."

Technically, both anglers were right. The jack salmon that surge into the tidewater sections of Oregon's coastal rivers in late summer (as early as mid-July in some cases) are of the chinook breed, though those which come in later are silver salmon.

By Oregon law, a salmon is not a salmon until it tops twenty inches, and at that length and beyond, anglers are required to punch the state-issued salmon tag that acknowledges a salmon catch. As far as the angler is concerned, however, a fish is a jack salmon if it is male, taken in tidewater before the first heavy rains of fall bring in the major adult salmon runs, and weighs less than ten pounds.

Nature plays a zany trick on jack salmon. Their milt sacks develop at sea at least a year too early, giving them the urge to join the upstream spawning run when they are still teenagers. Not knowing the score, they overdo it by coming in from the sea fully six weeks ahead of the main adult runs. Here they mill around in bewilderment, or have fun, depending upon how you look at it, since the water in the streams above tidewater is too low for them to continue the migration. The adult salmon, older and wiser, do not come in (except for a few early runners which mix with the jacks) until a heavy rain raises the streams for their migrating convenience.

Large numbers of these silver bright jacks (an estimated 10% of the total salmon run) mill about in tidewater fully six weeks before the main runs come in. Yet few anglers get into this fishing jamboree, since few know the secrets of the jacks.

How do I know when the jacks are in? As with the sea-run cutts, I have a ritual that I follow every year. Although jack salmon are prodigious jumpers, inclined to leap all over the place, they particularly like to jump on the turn of the tide that comes at bare dawn or dusk. Although there may be no sign of early jacks in tidewater during any other time, if you will journey to tidewater stretches of the rivers when there is a low tidal turn at dawn, or as full darkness comes down, you will see the jacks at play if they are in.

Always at such times you will also see, in particular holes year after year, an adult hen salmon or two leaping ponderously. As with the chicken and the egg, no one knows if the jacks come in first, or the few adults. We like to think that the amorous jacks follow early run females in with courting intentions.

Whatever the score on the above, these youngsters are silver bright at this time, fresh from the sea, with sea lice on their shingle-width tails, an angling prize on the line or in the frying pan. They are eager for fight or frolic, and now is the time to give it to them, before their silver sides darken and their marvelous fighting spirit dims. Anglers who meet these jacks upstream later, after the heavy rains, find them black-sided, hook-jawed, lean, feeble, and white-fleshed. It is difficult to imagine then what they were like in their prime just a few weeks previously.

Every year I arrive on the coastal streams at about the time I think the jacks will come in. When I see the huge, red-sided chinook hen, which always seems to appear in the Red Barn Hole of the Salmon River at this time, I know that the best angling of the year is at hand for me. When mentioning to Marion Huffman last summer that this huge chinook hen was jumping in tidewater, he looked at me with a twinkle in his eyes.

"I know," he said, gathering his gear together. "I could have caught her yesterday, but left her for this morning so she'd have time to grow a bit more. I doubt that she weighs more'n forty-five pounds now."

He was kidding, of course, for all confirmed jack salmon anglers know that this particular chinook is a chaperon for the young jack males, that she cannot be hooked, and she never dies.

It is certain that thousands of angler tourists miss out on jack fishing. They visit the Pacific coast on their vacations in summer and early fall, too early to hit the adult runs, which are at their peak in October. Yet from Mexico to Alaska, jacks come into tidewater and ascend rivers that have adult runs of either chinook or silver salmon. On rivers that have spring salmon runs, such as the Columbia and the Willamette, jack salmon may be taken in spring.

Everyone knows of the famed salmon runs of the coastal rivers, yet few know of jack salmon, which are part and parcel of these runs, know them, that is, when they are silver bright and in their prime. All salmon anglers encounter the jacks later, when they are black and half dead.

It is easy to overlook the jack salmon, as I did for years. Over thirty years ago I heard of the jacks while living in San Francisco, where they were known as *grilse*, the true name of young Atlantic salmon males.

I was told that if I journeyed north to the tidewater section of the Guallala River, I would find silver fish that would give me a real tussle. I went, and looked with disgust at the narrow placid tidewater section of the

Guallala. I did not realize then that, had I awaited a turning of the tide, had I been there at the time the jacks were jumping at play, I would have started my jack salmon fishing experiences years earlier. Instead, I turned away, feeling that I had been given a bum steer.

Not until five years later, did I start fishing for jacks in earnest on Oregon's Big Nestucca River. Since that time I have never missed a season, except when forced to during World War II. I have taken these splendid fish on rivers from northern Washington State down into California. I once parked my trailer house near tidewater on the Salmon River from July 26 to September 7, with my boat in the water meeting every turning of the tide. Since then, I have set up camp along the Salmon every year for weeks.

Much of my enjoyment of jack angling has to do with the angling method I use. It always carries me back to kid days with a willow pole and cork on the pond in the back forty.

There are many ways to take jack salmon, since they will respond to trolled or cast hardware, bait, and even sunken, gaudy streamer flies. But by all counts, and perhaps because it is merely different, taking them with a light rod strung with a plastic ball float brings the most fish and the most sport. You've never, even in your balmiest kid days, seen a float go down like a jack takes it down.

When that float cruises then disappears like a stone, the hackles stiffen on the back of your neck. It is something you can never witness casually, for you know that you are not about to strike back at a crappie or a bluegill. If you strike correctly you will be hooked to a fish that, for sheer power, will outfight any trout that swims save the great steelhead itself. Fishing for these lunkers with bluegill type gear really stirs up a rapid heart beat.

Without knowing the secrets of the jacks, an angler might easily get discouraged. I have sat in my boat while jacks beat the water to a froth around me, unable to get a strike. This can go on for hours. But the moment will come, and if you know when that moment is, you need not spend time waiting the jacks out. I often go to the jacks when I know they will not hit, just to watch them. Anglers who witness their playful leaping acquire a certain awed look in their eyes, and are never quite the same again.

Generally speaking, though, it is useless to go after jacks when the tide is flowing strongly in either direction, in or out. Jacks bite on the high or low turns of the tide, the low turn being best in my opinion. Of all times, a low tidal turn at dawn with a minus tide is best. I love slipping up the river at bare dawn, with fog wisps drifting over the water's surface and muskrat, beaver, and mink going about their business.

If you are fishing on a low or high tide turn, and you should be, take a bearing on some stationary object on shore, so that you will be able to detect when the tide stops rising or falling. Watch for the slightest *bulging* or *fading*. This bulging and fading occurs when the tide is still running in one direction along the bottom, and in a contrary direction (or remaining still) on the surface.

Jack salmon obey the hidden direction of the tidal flow. For instance, if you are anchored in your boat watching the tidal flow on a low tide turn, you will note that the water is still running out on the surface, while deepening on the twig you have marked with you eye, indicating that it is actually running in underneath. The jacks will be moving in on this submerged stream, and those already in will begin to hit. Now is the time to roll up your sleeves, freshen your bait, and prepare for action.

Sometimes the jacks only hit for a few hectic minutes on the tidal turns. Usually they hit when the tide begins to slow in its flow, before the turn, during the dormant period of the turn, and until the tide is flowing strongly

...to get out the familiar gear of childhood fishing and go for jacks.

after the turn. Other than at these times, you might as well go home. Very infrequently, the jacks will strike during heavy tidal flow, but not often.

If you are fishing a strange river without local advice, seek out the inside curves of the river's bends, where the water is deep and where it is less disturbed during swift tidal flow. If there be underwater snags here, so much the better. These snags, of course, make things very interesting when an angler is attached to a fish that has the power of the hind leg of a mule. The jack bores for these snags with real determination when hooked and is not easily turned.

Proper rigging of gear is very important. You must be equipped to cast far and accurately, for this is no game where you sit idly while your baited bobber floats. You don't dream in the sun when going for jacks at a time when they hit. You cast continuously, often to leaping fish. You let your bobber drift on the tide, reel it back, and cast again. You should be able to cast to all portions of the pool, and many tidewater pools are large. Moving the boat about is not good in jack fishing, unless of course, you are trolling with hardware. The anchored, bait fishing jack angler frowns upon disturbance in his pool.

To cast far and accurately with a gob of bait and a clumsy bobber, you need a special rigging. Use a light, whippy, seven-foot casting or spinning rod. Ten-pound breaking strength line is about right, although you may wish that it was stouter if you stash into an adult salmon, as often happens when jack fishing. But don't use a line so heavy that it inhibits accurate long-distance casting. Clamp a half-ounce sinker at the head of a two-foot leader, strung with a number two hook of finest quality. Above this attach a plastic ball float of about an inch and a quarter in diameter. Leave the line snap of the float open so that the float will move up and down the line easily.

About six feet up from the hook, loop a small rubber band tight enough that it can only be moved by a stiff pull with your fingers. Snip off the ends of the rubber so that the knot will pass easily through the rod guides in the cast.

When casting with this rig, the float remains at the leader head, above the sinker. When the cast lands, the sinker pulls the line down through the open bobber clasp until it strikes the rubber knot. Since the knot can't pass through the bobber clamp, this halts the downward sinking of the lure and gives the bobber a jerk that indicates to the angler that the bait did go down and did not become entangled during the cast. This is most important. The rubber knot can be slid up and down the line to achieve different fishing depths as the tide comes in or goes out. Pulled tightly enough, a rubber knot will last all season. If you can't manage the rubber lop-knot, make a knot by tying on many wrappings of silk or nylon thread.

Jacks are taken anywhere from right on the surface to ten or fifteen feet down. Usual fishing depths are six to eight feet. The bobber is essential for three reasons. It holds the bait from the bottom, where it would be continuously gobbled by mud cats or crabs. It permits the bait to drift with the tide. And it gives the angler indication of what the jack is doing below. It's also a thrill just to watch it go down! The bobber must slide to the head of the leader. Otherwise when you try to land a jack you can only reel in to the bobber, permitting your jack to run out of reach.

Trying to land a jack with a solidly placed bobber is akin to trying to sack up excited bobcats. You have more than a hilarious time, I assure you. These fish fight to the last fin beat. An angler can't get close enough to gill or gaff the fish. The acrobatic jack circles continuously. Recently I saw two anglers trying to land a jack on an exposed tidal mud bank. By the time they had the fish in hand, they looked as though they have been plastering houses with short-handled shovels.

Preferred bait for jacks is fresh salmon roe, though preserved roe will do in a pinch. Tackle dealers along the coast buy fresh salmon roe by the ton during the commercial fishing season to sell to anglers. The best roe is that which has been rolled in borax, then rolled up in newsprint. No other type of paper seems to do the job as well. Veteran anglers save roe from their female adult salmon, putting it up for next season's use by rolling it in borax and freezing it. The roe is cut into pieces the size of a nickle or a quarter, and is usually tied to the hook with red thread. I prefer to tie leader to hook below the bait holder notch, thus making a loop for holding the roe between bait holder notch and hook eye.

The strike of the jack can never be mistaken for anything else, once you have seen it. The float leans, cruises off, then simply disappears. You will have an overpowering urge to strike, but don't. Give slack line to permit the fish to take the bait fully in his mouth.

Striking against a slack line is a trick you have to learn. When the time comes, it must be done rapidly before the jack can reject the hook. Lean far over for a long heave, then reel in rapidly to get as near a tight line as possible. Now heave and follow through to overcome the resistance of the sunken bobber and give sinking power to the hook. Your rod tip must be limber enough to take the jolt if you misjudge striking distance.

Seeing jack novices attempt this long heave sometimes produces rib-trickling scenes. I have seen them turn backward somersaults out of their boats. One fellow I encountered last fall missed his fish and snagged into a set of salmon entrails that had been tossed into the water when a fish was cleaned. He gazed ruefully at the mess on his hook.

"Good Heavens!" he gasped. "I struck too hard. Jerked the insides right out of that one."

Having hooked your jack salmon, beware of the snags around you, and look out for their most baffling trick, which is to put on real power, then suddenly run towards you, handing you an armload of slack line. While you are trying to get a taut line, your jack may well get into the snags around the boat, for there are usually snags where they prefer to linger.

If he gets into the snags, give him slack line. Jacks have an uncanny way of getting out of the tangle themselves. Once you get a tight line on this toward-you run, you'll discover that this is not a sign of surrender. The battle is barely started.

Some chinook jacks jump and some don't. The silver jacks, which come in a bit later in the year, nearly always put on air acrobatics. Silver jacks can be distinguished from chinook jacks by a very narrow rim of white around the bases of the teeth in otherwise dark or black gums. Also, the dorsal fin of the chinook is black-dotted, while that of the silver is not. Silver jack meat is even redder than that of the chinook and, to my notion, a bit tastier.

One morning last year, I forgot to take my landing net out with me when after jacks. I hooked into a real jumper on the first bulge of the incoming tide, playing him amid the hazard of underwater snags. Reaching for the net, finding that it was not with me, I grasped the salmon by the lower jaw. He immediately went into corkscrewing contortions which lacerated my thumb on his teeth. I dropped him like a hot skillet, then tried to flip him into the boat with a gill hold, but only succeeded in tossing water into my face. Finally, in desperation, I unlimbered a short gaff and took him.

Sinking a gaff into silver-sided beauties such as this gives me a very sad feeling. Nine times out of ten you'll lose a jack if you attempt to hoist him into the boat by the leader. Maybe you can tail them, but I have little luck with this type of handling.

When your float goes down while jacking you never know when the strike may be from an adult salmon. The adults increase in numbers as the days run into fall. When this occurs on tidewater among the snags, you really have your hands full. I have landed many adult salmon, both chinook and silvers, while fishing for jacks in fall, but I have lost more than I have landed. I prefer to use a casting reel for jack fishing and, after a few experiences with line-burned thumbs, have formed the habit of taping my thumbs when going after jacks.

Chinook jacks average three to five pounds, the silvers somewhat less. I have taken jacks to twelve pounds, which anglers other than jack salmon fishermen would call adult salmon. But since these hefty fish are males and are found in tidewater before the adult runs come in, they're jacks all right. Adult chinook run up to fifty pounds, with any fish over twenty pounds considered a good catch.

I don't want to give the impression that I have a fishing riot every time I go out for jack salmon. I don't. There are days, as in all fishing, when it seems that all the jacks are still at sea. As a general rule, however, if you hit the tides right, know the best spots, and use the right gear and technique, you'll have a good chance of bringing home jack salmon steaks.

This is the golden time of year on the coast, where fall comes early. The air has a tang, and the tideland marshes lie still beneath a cool but golden sun. Blackberries hanging thick and sweet along the riverbanks can sustain an angler as he drifts by. Crows call from the firs, and migratory band-tail pigeons wing overhead. Ever present gulls scream with each tidal turn, and it's good to be alive. It feels good to get out the familiar gear of childhood fishing, the old plastic bobber, and go for the jacks.

They're beautiful in autumn, silver fresh from the ocean, one of the finest game fish that swims. In fact, jacks are the only game fish that I can take without regret. For when the rains come, the jacks make their heroic but futile run upstream with the main salmon runs, only to die, battered and spent.

The jack salmon run upstream does offer additional opportunities for some interesting angling. We will look into this type of jack fishing in our next chapter.

THE JACKS UPSTREAM

THE MOVEMENT OF THE JACKS FROM TIDEWATER into the rivers depends upon autumn rains. The light rain of August, which draws sea-run cutthroat into fresh water, comes too early to attract more than an occasional jack to the coastal streams.

After this early rain, the weather usually remains dry. Once again the Nestucca and the Alsea, the Wilson, Trask, and Salmon run low and clear, their music soft and muted. An outlander would detect no hint of rain in the offing. But weather-wise residents sense a coming change and speak of it with enthusiasm, preparing fishing tackle for what is sure to come.

A breeze springs up from the southwest. Low clouds form on the horizon and move in on the wind, blotting out summer's sun. Warm raindrops touch the placid surfaces of the pools, gently at first, then more fiercely. Rain sweeps across the forest, cleansing it, scenting the air with its pungency. Coastal rivers begin to stir. There is a quickening of the rapids, and of anglers' hearts. An ever-increasing volume of water begins moving down to join the ebb and flow of tides below.

First to feel this change are the jack salmon which have been milling about in tidewater. Some are already dark sided, their milt sacks bulging and ripe. Others, more recently in from the sea, are silver-bright. This is what the jacks have been waiting for. Rain pattering over their heads, and eager water flowing down to the sea triggers them into action. As one fish, they surge upstream, passing the head of tidewater and breasting into the rain swollen torrent. Alerted by the downpour, fishermen and women have rushed down to the river to meet the jacks head on.

At first there is a rather sorry harvest, for there are more dark, lean jack salmon in the water than bright specimens. But wait. With the first ebb tide, the flow of rain freshened water surges out to sea, where schools of jacks cruise in company with adult salmon. Salmon gill plates flare to the scent of rain. The schools turn landward. The fall migration begins in earnest.

After this second rain, which usually occurs in September, salmon anglers can choose their method and place of operation. They can fish for adult salmon in the bays and tidewater sections, fish in open water at sea, or move upstream. However the weather may vary from this point on, fishing has reached its autumn phase, and there's no going back.

The September rain is usually soon over. The rivers fall quickly, trapping the big salmon wherever they may be at the moment. The greatest numbers of adult fish will remain in tidewater until the next rain. But the jacks, better able to negotiate shallow water, will move upstream with a scattering of adults.

Anglers who desert the tidewater sections now to deftly fish the upper river face a time of selective fishing. No salmon fisherman worthy of the name wishes to take dark, spent fish from the water. Left in the river they perform their spawning functions and die. Their rotting flesh furnishes food for salmon fingerlings.

Dark salmon which retain full flesh, fat and firm rather than thin and hook-nosed, are still keeper fish fit for the frying pan. The test of fitness here is to hold the salmon aloft while gently squeezing the sides. If either milt or roe issues from the vent, return the salmon to the water unharmed. For this reason, a gaff should never be used on salmon at this time of year when there is a mingling of dark and bright fish in the river.

How long the above situation continues depends on how long the rains hold off. If additional fall rains are delayed, and the rivers return to summer low, salmon that have ventured upstream will grow progressively darker and leaner. Even during this period however, there is the opportunity to take a bright fish upstream, for a few venturesome jacks and adults will continue to fight their way up from tidewater during the hours of darkness. But with every rain, new fish will move in, until the full fall migration.

Most anglers employ steelhead drift rods for this kind of fishing, since it is more than possible to hook into an adult fish while going for jack salmon. We prefer to fish for jacks upstream with the lighter, more versatile equipment that we use for stream trout, particularly if the water has fallen to near summer's low. A light spinning rod, or fly rod equipped with a monofilament loaded free-line reel, capable of tossing a single buckshot with accuracy, is ideal for jack salmon on these brush-lined streams. If, in the course of events, an adult salmon does take hold of such gear, a fisherman can at least say that he had a time for himself!

To fish for jacks upstream, seek out the deep holding pools and the runs and pockets below such obstructions as waterfalls and boulder piles. Fish deep and slow when using bait. Salmon roe clusters or single salmon eggs, crawdad tails, and even night crawlers will produce well at this time. I have had silver-bright jack salmon come flashing up out of tiny pockets when the river was low after the first rain, take my bait and give battle.

When using artificials, cast them across and pull them through the pools. Wobbling plugs that have the orange coloration of crawdads and imitate the side-wobbling movement of swimming crawdads are among the best artificials for jacks in fresh water.

Most of the jacks in the streams in early September are chinook, but once another rain or two swells the coastal rivers, silver jacks will come in, thrusting their blunt noses into the torrent. Marion Huffman and I had an exciting time with silver jacks one October.

The radio that advised us that the coast would soon be treated to occasional showers. They may have been showers in the weatherman's book, but to us on the river they were torrents, roaring down upon the pools, transforming them into millions of tiny leaping jets as huge drops struck the surface.

Below the Rose Lodge Bridge, which crosses the Salmon River on the market road at the community of Rose Lodge, chinook and silver jacks were boiling in a steady stream through the narrow riffle at the foot of the pool. Water ouzels, so silent during most days of the year, sang from atop boulders, whipped by rain and wind, their throats swelling as though they would burst with joy, their melodies sweeter than that of the canary.

It was truly said by the late Ben Hur Lampman, beloved poet laureate of Oregon, that no man could rightly call himself a coastal fisherman until he had heard a water ouzel sing. Ben's statement was undoubtedly brought about by the fact that only those with the fortitude to be out on the coast rivers in a storm had any chance of hearing the song of this

94

They may have been showers in the weatherman's book...

intrepid bird. In over thirty years of fishing the Oregon coast, I have heard the water ouzels sing a number of times, and upon each occasion I have halted all operations to listen and marvel. Always the song came in the midst of the wildest rainstorms of the year.

There is something about the rains of the coastal country that makes them different from rains elsewhere. The day Marion Huffman and I faced the big rain on Rose Lodge Bridge Pool, the river was writhing in its channel like a demented thing, roaring as the water ouzels sang and salmon leaped. Today, having become a bit more salmon wise with my years, I would probably ignore the silver jacks on such a day, trying for adult silvers with a number four silver and brass spinner and a fluorescent yarn skirt, or a yellow wobbling plug.

But Huffman and I chose to cast small spinners in silver finish where the water curved down, cliff-bound, into the head of the pool. Silver jacks struck savagely with almost every cast. They leaped high as they felt the steel, and we landed them amidst the roaring spray and rain, the river's thunder dimming our shouts of excitement. We gloated over each fish, then took them to the river cabin where we rolled them in cornmeal and fried them in smoking bacon fat.

As I recall, this was the evening that Huffman, lulled into deep slumber by the rain drumming on the cabin roof, lost his false teeth to a one-eyed packrat. The beady-eyed beast was quite put out when we finally located its cache and retrieved the missing molars.

As I will point out later in the chapters on angling for adult salmon, chinook jacks should be fished slowly and close to the bottom, while silvers can be taken further up from the bottom. Jack anglers should also bear in mind that these fish are on a spawning run, swollen with milt, seeking female companionship and spawning gravel beds. Consequently they tend to lie upon gravel at the foot of a pool or run when the water is not rising with rain.

When the river is rising, the jacks often crowd eagerly into the entering flow in an effort to move higher upriver. To take advantage of this behavior, hit the tailings of pools during falling water, and the entering rapids during rain and rising water.

My favorite upstream jack salmon fishing spots lie along the Salmon River, from the headwaters of tide on up to above the second bridge. Any deep hole is worth working, even though it may only be a small pocket below an obstruction.

On the upper Siletz River above Taft, on the south shore of the Big Eddy Hole below Cedar Creek, there is a deep pocket where the jacks gather in numbers each fall. You can see them leaping at dusk. On the north shore of the Peg-leg Hole on the Big Nestucca above Hebo there is a jack hole from which I have taken these beauties in numbers.

The Little Nestucca offers many jack salmon fishing spots above Cloverdale after the rains. On the Little Nestucca silvers are more numerous than chinook. Other good jack waters include the Alsea, Ten Mile Creek north of Coos Bay, the outlet of Siltcoos Lake below Florence, the Wilson and the Trask. Any stream with a fall run of adult salmon also offers jack fishing after the first heavy rain of the season.

Fall jacks are not the only jacks of the Oregon country. Wherever spring and summer salmon runs take place, there are also jack runs. Along the Columbia and its tributaries, such as the Clackamas and the Sandy, I have found hot jack fishing in April, May, and June. Wendell Boyes, Newberg tackle dealer, told me of his experience netting jacks for anglers on Tanner Creek below Bonneville Dam on the Columbia, which kept him so busy he didn't have time to fish himself. Along the beaches of romantic Sauvie Island on the Columbia below Portland, jack salmon are taken each spring and summer in large numbers.

To me, the jack is a worthy opponent wherever found, but it's most choice when taken during Indian summer in the coastal tidelands, when the blackberries hang ripe and sweet from the vines, crows caw overhead, and band-tailed pigeons wing south. I don't know why this is so, for fast-water stream fishing is my favorite angling pastime with this exception. It's true that I get a tremendous kick out of taking leaping silvers in foaming rapids, but there is a certain flavor, an indescribable appeal, to bobber fishing for jacks in tidewater, when the sun is golden and the air is autumn cool.

Since anglers usually gauge the value of their sport by the size of the fish taken, I suppose I shouldn't rate jack salmon so high in my fishing book. Be that as it may, fishing for jacks stands high on my list among Oregon's angling opportunities.

Fishing for adult salmon is considered by all fishermen to be the ultimate in angling sport, whether at sea, in tidewater, or in the rivers. Men cross continents and even journey abroad for the privilege of trying for salmon. Along the Atlantic seaboard, where there are widely scattered numbers of Atlantic salmon (actually more closely related to our steelhead than to the salmon clan), people pay hundreds of dollars for memberships in clubs that control a few Atlantic salmon runs. But here in the Oregon country, folks fish for salmon as casually as they might for trout, perch, or bass. Here I have taken, and released unharmed, eighteen salmon during a single day's fishing. Having had a look at salmon youngsters, let's get out there with the adults of the breed, the chinook or king, and the silver or coho.

GOING FOR
SALMON AT SEA

ADULT SALMON CAN BE TAKEN IN OREGON practically ten
months out of the year by fishermen who know how to
go about it. Chinook salmon are available as early as
February in the Columbia and in some of the coastal
streams, such as the Trask, Wilson, and Nestucca.

Spring-run salmon, known locally as *springers*, are a
major sports fishery on the Rogue, Umpqua, Columbia,
and Willamette river systems. Angling for springers
extends into June, when offshore salmon fishing begins
to attract early-bird sportsmen. The ocean salmon fishery continues until the fish move into the bays and
upstream on their spawning runs. I have caught fall-run
salmon in coastal rivers as late as December.

Though I prefer stream fishing, I occasionally go to sea for salmon. Hot spots for this are at Wheeler on the Nehalem, Pacific City on the Nestucca, Newport on the Yaquina, Winchester Bay on the Umpqua, Depoe Bay on Highway 101 south of the Siletz, Coos Bay on the Coos, and off the mouth of the Columbia at Astoria. Anglers can use private boats or engage passage on coastal charters.

Although it does not require a great deal of skill to catch salmon at sea, it is thrilling to experience a hefty, acrobatic salmon leaping about on a long line in blue sea water. Slugging it out with a chinook in the ocean depths, from a seat in a sea-tossed dory, is a battle worth writing home about, believe me. Anglers who put to sea from coastal bays in small craft are a daring breed, willing not only to pit their skill against the salmon, but against wind and wave as well. A word of warning is indicated here.

Inexperienced seamen have no business putting out to sea in small craft, such as dory or rowboat, near the mouths of Oregon's coastal rivers. An angler unwise in the ways of coastal wind, weather, and particularly tides should always be accompanied by an experienced coastal fisherman, or be content to take passage on large craft skippered by licensed captains. Each year the sea takes its toll of the unwary and careless during salmon fishing time.

A good rule to follow here is to stay away from the mouths of rivers when the tide is flowing out. If you can see the surf breaking, you are in the wrong place! If you must be here at such a time, be sure to have an anchor capable of holding your craft should your motor fail. A sound dory is safe enough when the tide is flowing in. A schedule of tidal turns is available at all coastal sporting goods stores and docks, usually corrected for the river at hand. Crossing the river bars out to sea in small craft is a voyage that should only be undertaken by the vastly experienced. At the river mouth, on an outgoing tide, tide flow meets incoming breaker in a turmoil of water that no small boat can survive.

Tidewater on most coastal rivers extends miles inland into the Coast Range Mountains, affording ample water for the novice to negotiate without approaching the river mouths. For instance, the tidewater section of the Siletz River is twenty-five miles long; that of the Salmon River is five miles long; that of the Nestucca River is ten miles or more. I have boated the tidewater bays of these coastal rivers for many years without the slightest mishap.

Putting out to sea in a small craft, such as a dory, is a casual experience for those who know the ocean. To a novice it can be a hair raising adventure. Usually after the first attempt an angler either shuns such expeditions in the future, or becomes a devotee of this most exciting sport. I will never forget my first seagoing venture in a dory.

With Lee Crawford, prominent Salem attorney, I put out to sea in the pre-dawn darkness on a gray, foggy morning. We started out from the boat harbor at Depoe Bay in a Grand Banks dory which was eighteen feet long, driven by a fifteen horse outboard motor set in a well so that it would not be drowned out by following waves. The twenty-foot Pacific dory, built at Delake, Oregon, is highly regarded for this type of work, but Crawford had such admiration for the Grand Banks craft that he had his boat sent to him through the Panama Canal. Perfected by those horny-handed cod fishermen of the north Atlantic coast, it has served him well from the Columbia south to Port Orford.

We set out that morning from the snug harbor at Depoe Bay, driving the dory through the heaving channel beneath the Highway 101 bridge. As soon as we cut through the breakers we were met by the open sea. Long swells rushed toward us like hills rolling across a prairie.

We climbed the first comber and slid sickeningly down into the yawning trough beyond. Instantly the friendly lights on shore were gone. The highway bridge, the land, were gone.

We seemed to be lost in an endless expanse of mountainous water, riding a cockleshell. The eighteen-foot dory, which had appeared to be such a stalwart, heavy craft, now seemed very tiny and frail. To Lee Crawford this was an old and familiar story. But I had a sinking feeling in the pit of my stomach. Actually, with such a boat beneath us and Crawford's hand at the tiller, we were perfectly safe, but I didn't know this. I was uneasy.

"Better take a seasick pill," Crawford said. "You're turning green."

Actually, I have never been seasick, nor was I on this trip, but this is a problem for many seagoing anglers. Modern motion sickness medicine will prevent this malady in most cases if taken in time. I managed a weak grin as we approached the first bell buoy off Depoe Bay, a potbellied monster that rolled in the swells, emitting a clangorous funereal dirge. This did nothing to settle my nerves. Crawford attached a yellow-feathered jig and cast it out without any sinkers attached. Silvers hit close to the surface, while chinook are more often taken deep.

"Salmon aren't in this close, are they?" I asked.

"You bet they are," Lee said, as he heaved back on his rod.

Astern, a silver salmon leaped high out of the water. The reel handle spun in a blur of motion as the fish shot through the blue swells, leaving a trail of water smoke behind it. I made a dive for the cameras in the bow and began snapping pictures of the action. It was a show worth photographing. The silver is the flashiest fighter of the salmon clan. Here, in deep water, every twist and turn of the fight was visible in the clear depths.

Harbor Seal

Killer Whale

We climbed the first comber and slid into the yawning trough.

The seagoing salmon angler uses heavier gear than does the river fisherman. I detest the short, thick boat rods so often employed for this kind of sea angling. A proper rod should be at least six feet long, of bamboo or glass, with a double-handed butt and a star drag reel capable of holding two-hundred yards of twenty-pound line. The tip should not be board-stiff, but should be limber enough to give whip in the play to prevent tearing hooks out of the fighting quarry.

Quite often no sinker weight is used when trolling for silvers. When trolling for chinook, however, the lure should be taken deep by about four ounces of sinker lead attached several feet ahead of the lure.

Herring is so universally used today that many anglers have never made use of anything else. However, number four spinners with fluorescent nylon skirts, red and white plugs, silver wobblers, and other such artificials will still take salmon at sea.

Playing a silver torpedo while your small boat stands on end in the swells is a devil's dance to two-four music. The first fish that Lee Crawford hooked on our expedition off Depoe Bay made thumb burning runs that terminated in high end-over-end leaps. With the motor shut off and the dory wallowing in the trough of the waves, Crawford was spraddled out trying to stop a sizzling run when the silver turned and ran toward him. He was left with more loose line than he could handle for the moment. When he finally got tight line again he did a nice job of playing the fish. He got it in close, braced a knee against the gunwale as he sank the gaff, and heaved it aboard, a beautiful specimen.

"Why is it," he asked, "that the first silver of the season always seems to be the best?"

I knew how he felt. I had taken my first silver of the year many times, but always in the rivers or bays, never at sea. As I put my line out, a commercial fishing boat passed us, high mast and outriggers rocking in the swells. One moment I could see the entire ship; the next moment I couldn't see even the tops of the masts as the vessel went down in the trough.

I was roughly jerked back to reality by a yank on my rod. A salmon rose into the air astern and took off in the general direction of Japan. This seagoing silver streak took me to town so fast that I hardly knew what had happened when my line went slack.

"You hit him too hard," Crawford said. "We're trolling pretty fast. When you hit back hard on a strike the momentum of the boat turns your wrist snap into a heave. The mouths of these fish are much softer at sea than when they have been in fresh water for a few days."

We trolled on, using yellow and white feathered Japanese jigs with no extra sinker weight. The silvers hit these fast trolled lures near the surface with a vengeance. No hook setting heaves were necessary. A mile and more out from Depoe Bay we encountered a second buoy, a salt encrusted monster that danced a seaman's jig while emitting derisive hoots that seemed the most ominous sound I'd ever heard in my life. This was the last touch of civilization. Beyond lay thousands of miles of open ocean. Here, in a small dory, a man feels very inconsequential indeed.

"How far out do we go?" I called.

"Four or five miles, maybe six. Depends on where the main school is. Hand me a can of beer."

I handed him a beer, wondering if I'd ever see dry land again. Five miles out we ran into a rip-tide. This terrible looking maelstrom ripped through the sea with the exuberance of a galloping tiger. A rip-tide is the point where two divergent currents meet. Waves came at us from all angles as we ran this water inferno, arriving at last at a smooth slick of ocean that stretched up and down the coast as far as the eye could see.

We trolled this slick while wild waves pounded on either side of our narrow route. I hooked and lost four silvers to each one landed. Lee hooked two, landing both. I am sure that I lost my fish by poor handling. A hooked coho resents the steel with such enthusiasm that an angler has little time to recall what he did, wrong or right. I only know that I lost two silvers on the high jump, one on the deep squirm, one at the point of gaffing.

I was having a whale of a time, unaware of the passing hours. Here lies the fatal difference between the landlubber at sea and the real seaman. I didn't have a care in the world. But Crawford did. He was sniffing the breeze, looking to the sky, a wary look in his eyes. The wind had freshened. The long swells had changed to short, wicked chops.

"In a couple of hours she's going to kick up," Lee commented.

"Let's not be here," I said, "in a couple of hours."

As I spoke, the marching line of slick smooth water disappeared, wiped out as though it had never been. The jaws of the two lashing sides closed in upon us. There was no direction to the waves. They came at us from all angles until we got out of the immediate area. Then we drove north into the combers. The dory writhed and strained until I had difficulty holding my seat. The bow rose, slamming down into the troughs so hard that it seemed the floorboards would buckle.

"She's built for oars," Crawford said, "not motors. If we take it slow she'll bring us home."

We traveled steadily north into the wind. The dory climbed waves, poised a breathless moment, then dipped into the troughs. Each time the craft rose triumphantly. I watched, fascinated, by the dory's performance. Rough she might be, but seaworthy she most certainly was.

I kept wondering why we bothered to keep our lines out. Then a silver hit my lure. It leaped high out of the water on the crest of a following wave, then was gone. We ran into a school of black snapper which we boated from time to time. A seal rushed at us in the welter of waves and dove beneath the boat. A huge whale suddenly surfaced to the side. It blew a geyser of foggy spray high in the air, then disappeared.

Crawford commented, "I hope that that one stays clear. If he comes up under us it won't be nice."

Soon I heard the clanging of the first buoy, proclaiming the route to safety. That iron monster now seemed a friend in need. We rounded the first buoy and headed toward the clangor of the second. Land came into view again, waves breaking like bombshells on the rocky headlands, leaping high, falling back in cascades of foam. Beside us combers raced shoreward, lifting mightily in the shallows to fall in thunder. Somewhere in this maelstrom of water lay a narrow passage that led to the safety of the harbor. Miss it and you crash, or ground, or swamp; hit it, and you you are in God's pocket.

High on the shore, beside the highway bridge, were mounted two white painted columns, one before the other. On each was painted a perpendicular red stripe. The navigator maneuvers his craft so that these two red stripes line up, as one lines up the range finder of a camera. Then he comes in, knowing that he is riding down the channel. It is as simple as that for those in the know. We shot beneath the bridge into snug harbor. A fifty-foot commercial troller was tying up at the pier.

"Any luck?" Crawford inquired of the skipper.

"Not much," the captain said. "The fish are out there, but a man can't handle them in this sea. When she begins to turn white on top and tip over, I come in. After twenty years at sea I still get seasick, strange as that may seem. Say, Mister, you wouldn't want to buy this boat would you? She's sound, and I'll sell her cheap. When a man gets seasick after twenty years..."

"I wouldn't want to buy her," Crawford said, as he tossed our silvers on the dock.

That's silver fishing off the Oregon coast where, in my view, the ocean is more your opponent than the fish. One needs more of seamanship than angling skill. Fishing the bays is very different, but there, too, one needs knowledge of water, wind, and tide.

Approaching a coastal river bay when the salmon are in, I try to arrive at the last of the ebb to launch my boat or rent one. Boats for this kind of work should be at least fourteen feet long and sixty or more inches in beam. Be sure you have both oars and a well constructed anchor aboard, in addition to a dependable motor.

I like a rod of at least six feet, husky enough to handle a hundred yards of fifteen-pound line with an ounce of sinker weight and towing a number four spinner or sizable plug. You have a wide choice of lures.

In years past the favored way to take salmon in tidal bays was by trolling flashers, spoons, and spinners decorated with red feathers. Red yarn displaced the feathers when it was found that red feathers appeared almost black in water. Later fluorescent nylon yarn was substituted for wool. This proved to be superior to either wool or feathers for attracting salmon.

About 1952 anglers began using whole herring for bait. Known locally as *mooching*, this method of fishing for salmon created a boom in the sport both in the tidewater bays and at sea. Big sporting goods stores went so far as to hold evening schools to teach proper methods of hanging herring on the hook for trolling or jigging. Thousands of salmon anglers eagerly attended the classes. Various tricky rigs were manufactured for the purpose of holding the soft-fleshed herring in position, allowing them to "swim" like crippled fish.

The best method I've found, and the easiest for quick handling, is to cut off the herring head with a slant cut toward the back of the neck. Using two hooks, one tied firmly to the end of the leader, the other sliding on it, impale the sliding hook upward at the top of the cut, and the other near the tail, barb pointing forward. Now draw the leader slightly through the forward hook to give a very slight bend to the bait, causing it to wobble when put in motion.

Catch figures for salmon taken in sport began to zoom when the herring craze took over. In 1962, 237,811 salmon were taken by sports anglers, and the catch has been on the rise ever since. In July of 1965 I fished with herring off Westport, Washington and spent ten days fishing for salmon off Winchester Bay in Oregon, using herring alternately with spinners and plugs. Several salmon can be taken with herring to one taken with hardware lures.

All this appears at first glance to be a grand deal. But is it? Salmon angling is a sport that we want to enjoy and let our children enjoy after us. A salmon is a big fish, and one or two is enough to satisfy the appetite for weeks. The average angler of limited skill can take several salmon per season without the use of herring bait. If the use of herring brings about the slaughter of the salmon schools in tidewater and at sea, we might have slim pickings in years to come. I am against any method of taking game fish that is so effective that the future of the species is threatened. Whether this is the case with herring remains to be seen. Fortunately, Oregon has kept wary eyes open for the survival of the salmon runs.

Winchester Bay claims to be the world's best salmon fishing port. My wife and I once put out from Winchester on the Shamrock Two, a sleek twenty-eight foot vessel. We were after silver salmon off the mouth of the Umpqua River. It was late July. We were supposed to be out four hours, carrying six passengers. Within two hours' fishing time we had our limits of eighteen silvers, three per rod. This is an example of just how good salmon fishing can be off the Oregon coast.

Because we were fishing for silvers, which strike close to the surface, we trolled herring bait slowly, using four-ounce sinkers on short lines. Our catch was not phenomenal for the year 1965, for boats were coming in regularly with limits before their four-hour planned trip was completed.

When using herring for bait, remember that chinook salmon are inclined to feed deeper than silvers. Going for salmon on herring once at the mouth of the Columbia, I noticed that when I fished deep for chinook, the silvers struck right on the surface as I reeled up my bait to inspect it. Another time, when fishing on the Siletz Bay at Taft with a companion, my partner was using little sinker weight. Since the bay was alive with silver salmon and no chinook were being taken by any of the scores of neighboring boats that day, it was clear why I failed while Bob succeeded. I was fishing deep, right on the bottom, while Bob's careless handling of his bait caused it to be practically on the surface. This was another lesson to me to fish even shallower for feeding silvers than I had in the past.

On the above occasion, we had our boat anchored where the swift tidal flow was coming in before the breakers. Another method would have been to motor to this point, then attach a sinker heavy enough to hold the bait down on the bottom while we drifted, jigging the herring up and down. This method will take both chinook and silvers.

Herring is the prime lure for salmon near the mouths of rivers. These salmon are just coming in from the sea, or are moving back and forth between sea and bay, on the prowl for bait fish. Later, when they are farther upstream, spoon and spinner often work better than herring. The farthest from a river's mouth I have ever taken salmon on herring was five miles, except on the Columbia River. Salmon will take herring in the Columbia over a hundred miles from the ocean, because even at that distance the tidal flow affects the big river.

Salmon are creatures of the ocean's moods. They live by the tides as we live by the rising and setting of the sun. Salmon are more active and more inclined to feed on the turning of the tides than at other times. This inclination persists, I'm sure, even after the fish have journeyed beyond tidal movements. I have noted this effect on anadromous fish of all species in the Klamath River, a hundred miles from the sea, and in other rivers as well.

Recently I saw a chinook lying in the clear water of the pool below the Rose Lodge Bridge on the Salmon River. I sat on the bridge as the salmon lay motionless, a long dark shadow on the river bottom. The August sun lowered beyond the forested bluff, darkening the pool. I consulted my tide card, though this was not at all necessary. Here, when the tide turns from its last ebbing, four or five miles to the west, a cool breeze always springs up from the surf, pungent with its odors. Sure enough, when this breeze began to fan my cheek, the salmon below me began to stir. Soon it was cruising about in the clear depths.

CHINOOK IN FRESH WATER

TAKING CHINOOK IN FRESH WATER is a far cry from taking them while in a boat at sea or in the bays. This is salmon fishing at its wildest. You pull up your boots and get out there on the streams in all sorts of weather. You crash through thickets, crawl through brambles, get rain down the back of your neck, and generally have a wonderful time. When you hook a chinook, you stand and fight in your tracks until you win or lose. When a chinook takes the line and charges downstream with a fast river on its tail, you are on your own.

I used to meet a fellow on Oregon streams when the chinook were in who moved his lips in prayer when heavily engaged with a fish.

"It helps," he told me, straight-faced, "to call on one's God at a time such as this."

On most coastal rivers the chinook salmon, heavy-weight of the species, comes in first after the rains of fall, before the silvers arrive. What chinook salmon have done to me down through the years would have to be witnessed to be believed. The first one I tried to land forty years ago on the Salmon River took me for a ride, and I mean that literally. Standing in fast water to my boot tops, I tried to gill the beast ashore. The forty pounder swam between my legs and headed for deep water with me riding bronco. I dismounted in panic to save myself from a fast current.

On the Little Nestucca, twenty years later, I had a fight of two hours and three quarters with a forty-five pound chinook. Another chinook flipped me into the drink on the Rogue below Gold Ray Dam. And yet another slapped me in the face with a shingle-width tail on the Wilson, while a thirty pounder of unusual talents broke my rod on the Siletz.

While plowing about through bankside brush in fall, it is out of the question to carry along a landing net large enough to contain a salmon. Consequently, most salmon fishermen either land their fish by gaff, or by wrestling them ashore. Wrestling a chinook is akin to throwing a mule with a hind-leg hold.

This brings to mind the illegal gentleman from Arkansas. This character strolled down to the shore of the Big Nestucca where several of us were fishing. The water was fairly high and fast, but shallow enough over the riffle that the backs of the salmon could be seen as they fought the current. This long lean tourist from the Midwest observed our operations with a critical eye.

"You fellers," he declared in an Arkansas drawl, "are just plain wasting your time. Lend me that there hook a minute."

Without awaiting permission to borrow the "hook", which was a short-handled gaff, he picked up the lethal instrument and waded out into the fast water, wearing ordinary plowman's shoes. He socked the gaff into the tail of the biggest fish he could see. The results were astounding. The salmon took off in no uncertain manner. It stretched out almost horizontal to the water, then it suddenly reversed direction and drove back between the snagger's legs. His gaff arm followed the husky chinook with such force and speed that he turned a complete somersault, landing in the drink some feet upstream. If he hadn't let go of the gaff handle he would have been towed on his back down into the pool below. His action was illegal, of course, although as a newcomer he didn't know it.

"That fish," he declared, dripping like a wet seal, "is a heap stronger than one of Pa's mules."

Watching chinook anglers at work on the rivers over a period of time, you will note that some individuals take more fish than others. These fish takers are generally considered to be lucky. Don't you believe it. They may be standing among others, apparently fishing in the same manner as the others, but there's a difference. They know things that the others don't know, and use their knowledge. Luck is largely a myth in this business.

Success with salmon in fresh water requires a great deal of knowledge. You need to know the bottom contours of the stream bed, the travel and lying-in routes, what tackle to use, and how much weight or lack of it is needed to get proper control in the various strengths of current. While it's taken me thirty-odd years to gather what knowledge I possess about these fish, I firmly believe a more observant angler than I, who will look, listen, ask questions of those who know, and use the information obtained, can be fishing successfully in short order.

Of all the knowledge required to take chinook, the

most important is knowing the contours or the stream bed and the travel paths of the fish as indicated by the stream's currents and water depths.

You might suppose that such knowledge could only be acquired by an angler who lives near the stream, one who can become thoroughly familiar with it over a long period of time. This would rule out consistent success by the visiting angler. Usually this is the case. But I have developed a method that makes it possible for a fisherman new to the stream to quickly become familiar with its bed, current tendencies, and travel and resting areas. I will describe this procedure in our chapter on winter steelhead fishing, since reading the stream bottom is even more important in that fishery. Everything I say about stream bed reading in that chapter can be used for chinook angling.

Let us now gear up to approach the river. We're going after fish that have come into the river after the first heavy rain of fall. Fish of this species may weigh over ninety pounds. Nevertheless, the first thing to do is toss aside the heavy gear you may have used at sea or in tidewater bays.

Much lighter gear is the ticket in fast water, and for a number of reasons. Here you need casting accuracy that can be achieved with a twist of the wrist in close quarters, on streams overhung with trees and brush. You need a light line so that you will have minimum current drag in fast water, much preferable to using heavy sinkers to overcome the current's pressure on the line. Only with a light outfit can you put your lure where you want it and keep it there without too much bottom snagging.

Above all, you want a fairly light, fairly whippy rod tip. This will keep a wearying pressure on the fish without arousing it to panic when it is still fresh. With a light rod tip you can maintain this pressure and follow every move of the fish without tearing the hook out of its jaw or breaking the leader. Take my word for it, a heavy hand on a heavy rod is the last thing you want when you hook large chinook in fresh water.

I learned the lesson of light gear on salmon early in my experiences with this monster of the Pacific coast. Back in 1932 I was fishing for trout on the Rogue when I encountered a heavy run of chinook moving up through the riffles. Equipped with a five-ounce fly rod, a bit dubious about the outcome, I decided to attach a red feather skirted spinner to have a try for them. During the day I hooked eight chinook. Some of them took me to town. Others I was able to land. I am convinced that had I been using heavy gear that day, I wouldn't have hooked into those fish at all. If I had managed to connect with any, they would have turned downstream with disastrous results.

When chinook are first hooked, unlike their cousins the silvers, they seem to require a bit of time to think about it, to become aware of the fact that there is something wrong. They begin a fight slowly, though with tremendous power, if light gear and a light hand are used against them. Resist their power with heavy gear and a heavy hand, however, and the chinook panics. An all-out battle results, usually involving a downstream charge. Such charges, with the current on the side of the fish, are almost impossible to stop without breaking off.

On the other hand, fighting against light pressure, a chinook is inclined to fight in the pool. If it attempts to leave the pool, it is most apt to move upstream, so that the current works for the angler. Handling a big fish in this manner, an angler can gradually wear it down. When the downstream charge comes, if it comes at all, it occurs after the fish has spent most of its strength, and it can usually be halted without breaking off.

The ideal gear for salmon in fresh water is a two-handed butt rod with a long, whippy tip, not much heavier than that of a six-ounce fly rod. If you prefer to

117

use conventional gear, attach an easy casting, regulation level wind bass casting reel of the finest quality, strung with a hundred yards of hard-braided nylon, or nylon monofilament, twelve to fifteen pounds breaking strength. Take care, if using monofilament with this type of reel, that there is a close enough tolerance between the ends of the reel spool and the frame to keep the monofilament from slipping between the two parts, where it might be cut.

If you are using spin gear, use the same type of rod and strength of line. With the aid of the spin reel drag, line of two to four pounds less breaking strength can be safely employed, but do not use it when fishing near other anglers. A salmon pool can be ruined for the day by an angler who overestimates his skill or underestimates the salmon's power. I saw an angler hold up a pool once for seven hours on the Salmon River, only to finally lose the fish through a worn leader.

A two-handed butt rod permits me to lock the butt under one elbow and play the fish with one hand while resting the other. I prefer a rod butt that is not over twelve inches long behind the reel seat. This allows cross-arm casting, so that the butt will pass between hand and stomach without extending the arm. The result is accuracy without arm fatigue. My salmon rod tip is made of glass and is not much heavier than a six-ounce bass bugging tip. Overall rod length is seven and a half feet. I have taken hundreds of salmon on this rod, which is too light for bay trolling.

Let's get on a chinook stream. Time of day, and condition of water and weather control our actions. Our approach, we'll say, is to a pool where salmon are milling about and moving upstream after a heavy rain. If it is still raining and the water still rising, the salmon will be entering the pool at the foot and leaving at the head. This action will be more or less continuous through the day under such conditions. Fish anyplace in the pool now, with silver and brass spoons, plastic wobblers in red and/or yellow, and with spinners decorated with red or varicolored wool or nylon skirts, provided the water is not extremely clouded with silt. If it is very clouded, drift roe bait slowly and close to the bottom as you would fish for steelhead.

Let me say a few words about bait here. I prefer to employ artificials on chinook in fresh water. I use spoons, plugs, and spinners with nylon yarn skirts. I prefer this method because it pays off best for me. But if you've been told that Pacific salmon will not take bait when on the spawning run, I say baloney! They won't take herring or pilchard, as they did at sea or in the bays, but they will take salmon eggs, crawdad tails, even worms and flies.

With salmon taken consistently on bait every year, it is ridiculous to maintain that they will only strike at bait in anger. Yet many so-called experts quite often declare that this is the case. In clear water I have seen salmon approach roe bait lying motionless on the bottom, yards from their position, and gulp it down. Certainly this bait was not annoying them, not arousing their wrath! We can be sure that salmon do take bait when in the river.

Now, if the rain has stopped and the water has fallen or is falling, the fish will lie dormant in deep holes and channels, waiting for darkness before proceeding upstream. This calls for a different procedure. Using artificials, fish from the head of the pool, casting beyond the point where the salmon seem most apt to lie. Let the lure sink to the bottom, then pick it up to reel it slowly toward you. Get as close to the bottom as possible. Reel the lure very s-l-o-w-l-y toward you. The angler who reels his spoon, spinner, or plug slowly for chinook lying in a stream will take many more fish than one who reels fast.

119

Suit the size of the lure to the strength of the current. With a slow forward motion you can't speed up the wobble or spin of the lure, so you control action with size. A small lure, such as a small Russelure or Flatfish, will wobble faster in slow current on a slow reeling motion than will a large one. Watch your rod tip tremble, which indicates the lure's motion or lack of it. You want a fast-action lure, moving slowly and close to the bottom. Casting with hardware from the head of the pool or run is best. But in many instances trees and fast water make it necessary to cast from the side. In this case, cast the lure across and upstream. Let it move close to the bottom to swing around below.

When using bait such a salmon roe, use the same slow close-to-the-bottom drift that is used for winter steelhead, as described in following pages. Bear in mind that salmon in streams are on the spawning run, seeking to reach upstream spawning beds, which are usually closed to angling at this time by a wise Department of Fish and Wildlife. (There are also spawning beds used by salmon in the lower reaches where we fish, however.)

Early in the season the movement is ever upward on rising waters. It slows to hours of darkness on falling or fallen water. Therefore, fish all day for chinook when there is a good volume of water in the stream. Concentrate more on evening and dawn angling in low water, particularly when clear weather prevails. During these latter times, knowledge of the stream bed contours and currents, lying in and resting areas is most important. (See the chapter on winter steelheading for details of bottom mapping.) As the season advances, with the salmon ripening toward spawning, their tendency to lie on the gravel at the foot of pools and runs becomes more and more apparent.

The size of the chinook and the conditions where it was hooked control the length and difficulty of the battle. My toughest skirmish with a chinook occurred below the first falls on the Little Nestucca River out of Cloverdale. Marion Huffman and I fought this warrior for two and three-quarters hours.

Using my salmon rod, rigged with a new Langely bass reel and strung with fifteen-pound braided monofilament line, I had stashed into a forty-five pound chinook hen below the falls. This is an area which has since been closed to salmon angling. I probably used too much pressure at the start of the fight, because this fish tore off downstream through the fast narrow chute below.

Because of narrow quarters below the falls and a steep cliff, I was unable to follow the fish down. It went around the bend and out of my sight. Here it fought over shallow water before the riffle. With gravel close to its belly, it put on an amazing show of acrobatics which I could not see from my position, but which Marion Huffman observed with awe from his place on top of the cliff. From this observation point he shouted instructions to me. I shouted back, using so much voice over the roar of the falls that I was hoarse when the fight was over.

After an hour and a half my reel handle flew off. Marion came down to attach another one from an extra reel I carried. We then grew concerned about the line rubbing on the cliff. Huffman risked his neck climbing down the almost perpendicular cliff, hanging over fast, dangerous water, to get into a position where he could hold his hand against the line to prevent its being chafed on the rocky cliff face.

To my knowledge, no large chinook other than this one has ever been landed here after it went down the chute below the falls. We finally managed to work it upstream enough for Huffman to sock home the gaff, hanging precariously to the face of the cliff as he did so. Needless to say, I could not have landed this one alone.

My second toughest chinook battle occurred in company with the same Salmon River veteran. This time Huffman hooked the chinook, a fifty-one pound buck, while I did the honors of aiding him. This fish turned upstream with such power that he was in danger of running Huffman's reel fresh out of line, a hair raising experience with a chinook, which can break almost any weight line if allowed to come to its end.

I charged upstream through brush and brambles to get above the salmon. I could see him down in the green depths, fifty-one pounds of muscle. I threw a rock in front of his nose, which caused him to torpedo downstream in no uncertain manner. On the way down, he passed the line around a sunken snag on the far side of the river.

Huffman immediately put on the lightest possible pressure, which caused the salmon to rest below in deep water, allowing Huffman to wade up opposite the snag. I then went below and cast over his line, entangling my sinker around it. I moved down the bank until I had slid my entanglement down to the head of his leader. Then I began to play the fish from the side while Huffman released line from above!

This was the salmon battle of the century. Spectators gathered to watch the action. Finally, in one of its lateral charges, the chinook rammed its snout into the weeds at the nigh shore. An alert bystander socked a gaff into its tail before it could back away. This fellow would have been dragged into the drink if another bystander hadn't grasped him by the back of his belt as he began to topple. Working together, the three of us managed to slide the chinook up on the bank. It was so heavy that we couldn't carry it to the car. We had to drag it. It was a bit dark, but was fat and prime.

All salmon anglers should remember that dark fish which have become lean, and which will emit roe or milt when their sides are gently stroked, should be returned to the water if uninjured. Such fish are poor eating, yet are worth their weight in gold in the stream. On the other hand, darkness and loss of the silver brightness of

Huffman was hanging over fast, dangerous water...

the sea do not reduce the eating quality of salmon if they are still fat and not lean-jawed. Their flesh will still be rich and red, while lean, spent fish have white, colorless meat.

Personally, I never remove an uninjured dark sided salmon from the water, but then I am constantly on the streams and am not as hungry for salmon steaks as some other anglers might be.

How tough and drawn out a chinook battle might be is highlighted by another experience of mine on the Salmon River at the Leaning Tree Hole. This tug-of-war occurred in the same run where Marion Huffman and I fought the fifty pounder early in the season. I hooked this fish in fast water after a heavy rain, using my usual light rod strung with a hundred yards of fifteen-pound breaking strength monofilament, backed by fifty yards of linen.

I fought this fish for two hours and ten minutes, timed by my wristwatch. During this time I did not see the fish. The salmon, which I judged to be the largest I had ever hooked, made four downstream charges during the engagement. Each time I did what must be done to meet such maneuvers, when brush and trees prevent following the fish downstream. I *turned him loose* by slacking off line. This tricks the salmon into thinking that it is free. Keep the pressure on at such a time and the fish will continue to drive home the charge. Slack off line, and it usually will stop, then turn around and come back upstream. On this occasion the hook pulled out on the fourth downstream run.

It might be said that I would have landed this salmon with heavier gear. I do not agree. With a heavy line I would have had so much current drag in the fast water that I probably would not have been able to make a slow drift to hook the fish in the first place. The salmon would have reacted even more powerfully to heavy gear, and the hook would have torn out quicker.

There is no greater fighter in fresh water than the royal chinook, for sheer power and dogged battle. The silver salmon, on the other hand, is faster and more inclined to jump. It puts on a dazzling show. For my money, there is no fish taken in fresh water, not even the acrobatic steelhead, that will put up the scrap of a silver in its prime. Sink the hook into a chinook, and it lies there a few moments, making up its fishy mind that there is something decidedly wrong, and that it should do something about it. The silver, or coho, explodes at the touch of the barb. It literally blows a hole in the water upon the instant of hooking.

Contrast the chinook battle described above with the fight of a silver in this same type of water. A silver would have gone into the air at the touch of the barb. It would have fought faster and with more rushing around. In this way it would have exhausted its strength more quickly. I have seen silver salmon on many occasions jump across pools, landing from the last jump when the holes from the previous ones were still open on the surface. I have seen them continue these jumps until they bounded out of the water on the far shore. I have seen them cavort across rivers to leap into over-hanging shrubbery.

The chinook is a bulldog type fighter. The silver is an acrobat. The successful chinook angler is not necessarily a successful silver fisherman. Let's go down to the river where coho leap in the riffles.

SILVERS IN FRESH WATER

SILVER SALMON, ALSO KNOWN AS COHO, are the fastest
fighting salmon of the Pacific species. At times they hit
savagely at properly presented lures. At other times,
though thick in the stream, they seemingly refuse to hit
anything. But even at such times they mill about, jumping thunderously. Whatever their mood of the moment,
they always put on a good show for the angler fortunate
enough to be streamside when they are in from the sea.

My wife and I have had two experiences with silvers
on the Oregon coast that highlight the striking and
nonstriking moods of these great, silver fish. On the
Little Nestucca, up high where this stream flows
through green meadows and towering fir forest, we
found silvers cavorting in the crystal waters in teeming
numbers. It was a brilliant, sunlit autumn day, one of

127

those days when it is a joy to be alive in the Oregon coastal mountains. The coho leaped in the pools, cruising so close to the surface that they made V-shaped wakes on the water. Casting across these pools, we felt our lines move over their bodies. Yet during the entire day, we didn't get a single strike.

As evening shadows slid across the water, the restless silvers of the pools began to move upstream through the shallow riffles. They shot through like atomic torpedoes, in many cases with most of their bodies out of the water. We waded out on a narrow riffle where, howling with laughter and excitement, we tried to head the salmon off as one would herd chickens or hogs. The salmon simply refused to be shooed back. They dodged this way and that, shot between our legs, upset us in the drink, and went their way.

Though we didn't get a strike that day, looking back we consider it to be one of the best days of our lives. There is something awesome and exhilarating about the upstream migration of a school of salmon.

The other experience with coho which comes so vividly to my mind occurred on the Salmon River, where silvers were also before us in numbers. These, however, were in a savage striking mood. I saw an angler hook twenty-six silvers that day, though without landing one. Meeting multiple jumps and wild downstream charges, this fisherman wended his way home at dusk fishless, an astonished and bewildered individual. I was testing a braided multifilament line that day for a large manufacturer of angling equipment. The silvers quickly proved that this line should not be released for sale. It never was.

On lesser fish it might have passed the test with flying colors. It had tensile strength, but could not take a quick snapping blow. In ten-pound breaking strength, it handled my first silver well, until the enthusiastic specimen torpedoed downstream in white water below

VINE MAPLE SMOKED
SALMON

SILVER SALMO
TRASK RIVER

We felt our lines move over their bodies.

the pool. With thumb bouncing on the spool, I let him go, hoping to slow him without breaking off, then put on the pressure. If I couldn't stop him that way, I planned to *throw the line at him*, to turn him loose so that he would feel free, turn about, and come back.

But he sailed into the air, end over end over the white-frothed rapid. There was the terrific splash of his landing, then he took off downstream like a tail-burned bobcat. The action was so fast that he caught the line flapping loose in the air from the jump, snapped it taut, and popped it like sewing thread.

This line would take a ten-pound pull, but would snap on less than a five-pound snapping jerk. This suggests the best way to test salmon and steelhead lines. Pull them with your two hands, somewhat under breaking strength. Now move your hands inward a couple inches; put a snap strain on the line. Lines that cannot take this test have no place on a salmon or steelhead stream.

That was a wild, wonderful day on the Salmon River. The air was ocean-scented by the softly falling rain, and the wind showered golden alder leaves into the pool. The fish were constantly on the move. They shot up through the riffles at the foot, leaped in the depths, and climbed the rapid at the head. On such days when the silvers are in, an hour is but a minute, and the day passes swiftly from first light to dusk.

Why did the salmon of the Little Nestucca refuse to strike, while those on the Salmon River struck savagely? The answer, I'm sure, lay in the weather. On the Little Nestucca the day had been bright and sunny, the water low after the first rain. On the Salmon, a storm was in progress, with the river rising.

But we mustn't try to tie silver salmon actions down to any hard and fast rules. I have known them to hit on sunny days and refuse to do so in the rain. I would say, however, that an angler's chances are better on stormy or dark days. I believe Laurel and I would have taken silvers that sunny day had we arrived streamside at dawn instead of when we did, with the sun high.

If there is any hard and fast rule that we can attach to coho angling, it is that they will bite most enthusiastically at gray dawn. When the silvers are in, regardless of the weather, I usually can take them at dawn, even though they may not strike at any other time that particular day, even at dusk.

My New England bred mother had a theory about cheese and apple pie which she often quoted. "Apple pie," she would say, "without cheese is like the kiss without the squeeze." Silver salmon angling without rain and storm loses much of its exquisite thrill. Falling rain, a roaring river on the rise, wind in the firs, and silvers leaping in the riffles just seem to go together like Mother's cheese and homemade apple pie. With rain spray on your face, a throbbing rod in your hand, and the roar of the river in your ears, you are really living, that is, if you are a fisherman.

Let us compare angling for silvers in fresh water with angling for chinook in the same element. We employ the same gear, and the same lures (except that silvers seem to prefer yellow artificials, while chinook prefer red). Silvers take flies far more readily than do chinook. The best flies are two or three-inch streamers of yellow and white bucktail. For silvers, try tying a two-inch length of key chain along the streamer wing to act as a weight to take the fly down, and as a metal attraction.

As for bait, silvers will take the usual chinook baits, but are far more partial to single salmon eggs than are chinook, which seem to prefer large gobs of salmon roe. One should fish slowly for chinook, close to the bottom. Silvers circulate more in the pools and runs and can be

131

taken at any depth. And they announce their positions more boldly by their greater tendency to jump in play.

To fight silvers, use the same semi-light gear that is best for chinook in fresh water. This will give ease of casting and accuracy, control in the current cross threads, and swift but light response to the silver's lightning-like combat. Heavy gear simply results in torn out or straightened hooks.

Coho open the fight instantly when they feel the hook. They are far more inclined to charge downstream than chinook. When you stash into a coho, you have your hands full. You put on all the pressure you dare—and pray. Here the long, light, and whippy rod tip means everything. It follows the play, giving easily with strain, and prevents breaking the line in a way that no heavy rod tip could.

I will never forget the time a newspaper photographer from Portland came out to my home, which was then on the Salmon River, to photograph my handling of silver salmon. Together we went down to the river at gray dawn.

Silvers were leaping at the end of a tongue of fast water. I hooked one at once on a yellow Russelure. This fish, a fifteen pounder, put on a real show for the camera. It simply tore the pool apart, jumping here and there in bewildering fashion. Its maneuvers became so fast and confusing that I fumbled the play.

Suddenly reversing direction, the silver ran toward me, handing me an armful of loose line that I didn't know how to handle, since I no longer knew where the fish was at the moment. Reeling fast to locate the salmon and to get taut line, I made a fatal mistake. I permitted my rod tip to develop a circular movement which tossed a half hitch around the end guide. The silver, which proved to be upstream, now shot downstream. It came to the end of the line and popped it as if it were no more than a piece of twine.

The speed of these fish is utterly fantastic. You deal here with a fish that will either snap the line or rip the hook from its jaw if it catches you, for even a fraction of a second, unable to pay out line. For this reason I always fight salmon with one hand, with my double-cork gripped rod locked under one elbow, my thumb on the reel spool.

With the rod locked under an elbow and playing the fish with one hand, I have two advantages. The single arm can move rapidly in any direction to extend or retract the rod to meet rapidly developing maneuvers. Also when one arm tires, the rod can be shifted to the other. I have gone to bed at night upon many occasions with my arms aching from long drawn-out salmon battles.

When fighting a salmon with one hand, I use the other to take in line, but only when the fish gives in to the stiff bend of the rod. I never try to use more force on a salmon than the fully arched rod will deliver. Spin fishermen have the drag on their reels to aid them when handling heavy fish. The rod you use is a matter of choice. For this type of fishing I prefer the conventional casting reel, for no reason other than that I've had more experience with it on large fish.

Unlike chinook, silver salmon usually come into the river in schools, rather than dribbling in by twos and threes. One moment a river may be barren, and then suddenly the silvers are present in numbers. When they are moving upstream, it is a good idea to fish for them just ahead of the rapid at the foot of the run or pool. The more husky, slower moving chinook is not as apt to strike in this fast water as is the silver.

Hooked here, however, the silver is in a prime position to hightail it downstream. When this occurs, the fisherman is hard put to stop it. Quite often this leaves an angler standing somewhere around the bend as line melts from his reel, unable to do anything but watch in dismay. The spin fisherman doesn't dare tighten the drag, nor does the casting reel angler clamp down hard on the reel spool, for fear of popping the line.

In such predicaments the best technique is to slack off on the line completely. Often the salmon feels that it is free, and turns around to come back upstream. This maneuver sometimes saves the day. To halt a charge before it gets well under way, the reel spool should be tapped with the thumb alternately, as you would tap the brake pedal of a car in a skid. This delivers thudding jolts to the fleeing fish and often discourages the run. If this doesn't work, there is no recourse but to throw the line at him and hope for the best.

It is not that unusual to have a silver that is attached to the rod of an upstream angler suddenly jump in your face. I have had this occur when I couldn't even see the other fellow, and was mystified as to what was going on. In the Peg-leg Hole of the Nestucca I watched a silver jump all over the place before discovering it was on a rod far upstream.

This phenomenon has become more frequent since spinning reels have been built to take two or three-hundred yards of monofilament. The usual practice is to set the reel drag just under the breaking strength of the line, then to hang on, letting the drag do the work. With light lines and light-set drags becoming the rule among spin casters, there are more characters dashing around in the brush streamside hooked to runaway salmon than can be counted. With silver salmon there is always a good show on the coastal rivers of the Oregon country!

The Columbia River and all the coastal streams have silver runs in the fall. Some of the coastal rivers are hotter for silvers than others. I like the Little Nestucca; the Siletz, at Taft; the Salmon, at Rose Lodge; and Ten Mile Creek, north of Coos Bay. But any coastal stream will produce for those who get out there often.

At times the outlet at Devil's Lake at Delake, the D River (claimed to be the shortest river in the world) puts on a show that is well worth seeing. This stream is hardly a hundred yards long from ocean to Devil's Lake outlet. During times of heavy surf when the silvers are coming in, waves carry the fish into the face of the outlet. When the waves recede the fish are left flopping on the sand. I have seen them shoot about in scant inches of water, plowing sand as they go. At such times police are stationed to prevent bystanders from rushing out to engage in hand-to-hand combat with the fish. It is illegal to take silvers from the D River below Devil's Lake. They can be taken after they enter the lake, however.

The same rules regarding water height and lure coloration hold good for silvers as for chinook. I like yellow for silvers. A yellow or yellow and white wobbling plug, or a brass and nickle spinner decorated with a yellow skirt of fluorescent nylon material are my favorites.

When I have silvers before me and the water rising with rain, I generally take a position halfway down the pool, casting across and upstream, letting the lure swirl down to a point just ahead of the rapid at the foot. I hold it there, sweeping it back and forth with a movement of the rod tip. Silvers entering the pool or run are very apt to snap at the lure in passing. I don't try to get the lure as close to the bottom as I do when fishing for chinook. I keep it deep, but depth is not as important as color and action.

A deft hand is required when using the single salmon egg for silvers. This a good method when the water is high and roiled. So light is the silver's strike on a single salmon egg that the fisherman must sense it rather than feel it. How delicate this strike is was brought solidly home to me on at least two occasions.

I was fishing with companions on the upper Little Nestucca River. One of my companions was Wendell Boyes, a Newberg tackle dealer. Wendell is an expert in single-egg angling for silvers, as he proved by hooking fish after fish. These were extremely wild fish which shot across the river in a series of jumps, often leaping out on the far bank. Wendell was losing most of them, but having a wonderful time. I was photographing the action. Our third companion, a walnut grower who shall remain nameless, was complaining that Wendell was very lucky. The walnut grower couldn't get a strike, even when his bait lay within inches of the very spot where Wendell was hooking fish.

"Stop complaining," Wendell told our comrade. "You're getting strikes all the time, but you don't know it. You're not feeling them."

"Bosh!" the walnut grower protested. "I haven't had a nibble since I got here."

"You've got one biting now," Wendell cried out, pointing. "Sock it to him, man!"

Our companion lifted his rod tip. A silver leaped straight up, almost into his face. It shot across the pool, leaped several times, and threw the hook.

On another occasion, when fishing below a sheltering bridge on the Salmon River, my wife and I saw a fisherman whose inexperience was indicated by the short bass-casting rod he was using. He lost several silvers on single-egg bait. On three occasions he raised his rod tip to inspect his bait and, unknowingly, light-hooked silver salmon. The first two fish merely shot away, throwing the hook. The third fish, however, broke the bass rod off at the handle, then took handle and reel away from the fellow. I have never seen a more bewildered angler in my life.

The strike of the silver on a single egg is so light that there is a barely perceptible trembling of the line, with perhaps a slight quiver at the rod tip. Wrist snap the hook home at such times. Often you will be agreeably surprised.

Whatever may be said about bait angling for coho, the most satisfactory way to take them in the rivers is with artificials. The strike is not difficult to detect. It comes with smashing power. And when you beach a fat, streamlined silver salmon you have a real prize in your hands. The flesh when fresh is a deeper red color than that of the chinook, though the chinook retains its color better when canned. Canned coho is a treat on anyone's table, particularly if it has been smoked a bit with vine maple before canning. Ambrosia!

In the coastal country of Oregon there are several sportsmen's canning plants where you can have your salmon custom canned and labeled with your name and the stream where it was taken. I usually have my fish canned at Depoe Bay, or at Winchester Bay on the Umpqua River. Salmon so canned is better than the canned salmon bought in stores because its fresher by a long shot, and because salmon taken from the rivers are more flavorful than salmon taken at sea.

Around the anglers' cracker barrel I can bring about hot arguments by maintaining that the fighting silver salmon is more sporting on the rod than the steelhead trout. Though I take the side of the silver, I do this perhaps because I love him so, because I have so often seen him leap on my line in a lash of spray, flashing in midair like the blade of a saber. Nevertheless, I must admit that the steelhead, matching the silver pound for pound and often heavier, is the all-around champion of the trout breed.

If it is a fight that you want, a fight that drives your heart into your throat and sends cold chills running down your spine, the steelhead will give it to you. This is the fish that eludes persistent anglers for years. I have known men who have failed to take a single steelhead in years of trying. Yet steelhead are quite easy to take if attention is paid to the details of the game. There are certain techniques that must be mastered before you can have consistent success with steelhead. Let's go steelheading.

WINTER STEELHEAD

CHINOOK CAME INTO THE COASTAL RIVERS with the fall
rains. Later, silvers swept in from the sea to cavort in
the riffles. I had enjoyed good sport with both. But now,
with the last days of October at hand, I had seen it all,
the coming and fading away of the year's salmon runs. It
had been wonderful, but now it was nearly over.

The hillsides along the river blazed with crimson
vine maple. Alder leaves had long since turned to gold
and faded to yellow, their tattered fragments tossed into
the pools and runs, clogging the rapids. The chinook had
deposited their milted roe in the redds of the gravel bars
and were now old and dark, spent and dying on the
deer-trampled sandspits.

The silver sides of the cohos were turning red, their
pugnacious jaws leaned to boniness, as are the jaws of

men who have lived too long. Yet there were still a few bright silvers in the pools. I stood there in the rain in my dripping slicker, casting to them.

I cast dispiritedly, with a sense of loss that the golden days of fall were about gone, not to be enjoyed again for another year. As I pondered this, a fish hit my lure where I had cast it into the rain swept torrent. I set the hook, and the fish leaped high in the air, tumbling end over end, bright as a silver sword. I drew in my breath and yelled.

"Fish on! Clear your lines. This one's a steelhead."

That's the way it happens each year on the coastal streams of the Oregon country. To heck with the salmon; the steelhead are in! The man who takes the first steelhead of the season on each coastal river feels ten feet tall. One season this happened to me on the thirtieth day of October, on the Salmon River.

I was fishing fifty yards above the Rose Lodge Bridge in a small, very swift pocket in the rapid. When the fish hit I thought it was a silver. When I set the hook, it torpedoed downstream so fast that I couldn't give enough line without bringing a backlash to my reel. There was nothing to do but run with the fish.

I ran full tilt, raincoat flying in the breeze. As I ran I yelled a warning to a fellow who was fishing below where the swift current broke off into the depths beneath the bridge. The fisherman stood hip-deep in the current, looking back at me with a puzzled expression in his eyes. Then he saw the huge fish rushing at him, about to pass between his widespread legs.

This fellow proved to be a man of quick decision and action. He clamped his legs together, and as the fish passed him, brushing against his boots, he ducked and threw the line over his head. This cleared me for the play. I bounded past him, then came up against the cement abutment of the bridge. I could go no farther. I had to stand and fight.

bump the bottom

"Fish on! Clear your lines. This one's a steelhead."

I'll never forget the moments I spent plastered there, chest tight to the cement while I bore down on the reel spool, releasing line a bit at the breaking point in an attempt to stop the run without breaking off. I stopped the downstream charge at the lip of the break-over from the pool, worked my fish back, and finally played it down.

This was the largest steelhead I had ever taken up to that time. It measured thirty-eight inches long and weighed over twenty pounds. It was the first steelhead taken from the Salmon River that year. I loaded it in my car and drove around to show it to my friends. Men who had put away their salmon rods got them out again and headed for the river. The steelhead were in! Good fishing was now assured through March.

Each year I meet many anglers who are eager to take one of these most prized of all trout. I try to explain to them how it is done. In order to explain, I feel that I must tell them of the years I spent fishing for steelhead without success. In this way I become a kindred soul, a person who has suffered the same defeats as they have. So they listen to what I have to say. Otherwise they might consider my remarks just so much streamside gabble.

I tell them of how I climbed into the Green River gorge way back in 1922 to try my hand at steelhead fishing. And I tell them of the times I drove hundreds of miles each fall from southern California to fish the Klamath River. I tell them of all the times I was skunked while others beside me took fish. Then I try to tell them what to do. Sometimes it works out well.

Angling for winter steelhead in winter swollen waters, we are not so much trying to defeat a fish as we are attempting to defeat the elements in which the fish swims. It is the swollen water that makes the game rough, not the wariness of the steelhead. Knowing this

142

takes the mystery out of the business. Steelhead fight like a demon, yet hit as gently as a perch.

The steelie lies close to the bottom. It will seldom turn to chase a lure that passes far from its snout, or passes too swiftly. So our problem is to achieve a slow, close-to-the-bottom drift in water where steelhead are inclined to lie, rest, or feed. Manage this, and the problem of taking winter steelhead is solved.

It seems simple, but it is not. Yet knowing what must be done, we no longer work without purpose. Above all, we no longer talk of luck in connection with winter steelhead fishing, for we know that luck has nothing to do with it.

There is considerable knack in achieving a slow, close-to-the-bottom drift in high, fast water. The technique requires a fairly long and limber drift rod. This should be strung with the lightest line the angler feels capable of using on such powerful fish. Eight pounds on spin gear and ten pounds on casting gear is about the right breaking strength.

The sinker is most important. It should be just heavy enough to *kiss* the bottom in the drift, yet not so heavy that it hits and snags frequently. For this reason steelhead anglers should always carry a variety of sinker weights, changing to suit the various current strengths.

Snagging in this type of work is always a hazard. If you don't hang up on the stream bed occasionally, you are probably not drifting your lure deeply enough. Your terminal tackle should be rigged so that when you do hang up, you will lose only the sinker. There are several methods of accomplishing this. A popular method is to attach various lengths of *pencil lead* to the head of the leader by thrusting them into the end of a hollow rubber tube. I leave two or three inches of leader material thrusting out at the head of my leader. On this I clamp eared or split shot sinkers with my pliers, so that they

143

will pull off easily. When the sinker is bumping bottom, the lure will swirl up above at leader length. Too long a leader raises the lure too high above the steelhead.

Equipped with the proper rod, weight of line, and sinkers, the smart steelhead fisherman seeks out those long, fairly deep and swift drifts in the river. Above all, he seeks water that has a considerable amount of hard-to-negotiate water below it. In all the steelhead rivers I have fished, and I have fished most of them from the Strait of Juan de Fuca to central California's Russian River, the pools and runs that produce the best have been above water that was difficult for fish to climb. The water above serves as a resting pool, at least temporarily, for fish fighting their way upstream from the ocean.

You may ask, why all this drifting business? Why not just plunk the lure out there and let it lie? Plunking is a pleasant, lazy way of fishing, best accompanied by an aromatic fire and a steaming coffeepot. Plunking for winter steelhead pays off when the fish are moving upstream in numbers. But it does not pay off as well, nor is it as thrilling a sport, as casting and drifting. Steelhead are a fast-water fish. They are seldom found loafing in a pool or eddy, the type of water most suitable for plunking. Your chances are much better if you seek them in the rapids, covering a great deal of water by drifting your lures.

All sorts of lures are used in the drift. Salmon roe bait the size of a quarter is most common. Other popular baits include fluorescent pink yarn, artificials manufactured to imitate salmon roe, and wobblers, spoons, and spinners.

The lure is generally cast across the stream, with slack line given the instant it lands so that it will sink quickly. If the sinker does not kiss the bottom every few feet, it is drifting too high. Put on more sinker weight. Each time the sinker bumps the bottom, give the rod tip a twitch. This keeps the sinker rolling. To drift through a long stretch of water without the terminal gear coming to shore, take care not to let the line tighten against the lure. The knack here is to give line as the lure drifts without letting it tighten, yet keeping it tight enough that you can feel everything going on below. This is a very difficult technique to describe, one learned by experience.

Always bear in mind the delicate nature of the strike of a winter steelhead, particularly on bait, or lures that imitate bait. It is a strike that fishermen often have to sense rather than feel. A steelhead quite often picks roe bait up in its mouth and drifts with it while sucking it out. It then drops the egg husks. If the drifting sinker is bumping along the bottom of the stream, then suddenly does not bump—strike! Every season I see novice steelheaders re-baiting hooks which hold sucked out egg husks, not realizing that they have had steelhead strikes.

I was taken in by this bit of steelhead strategy a couple of years ago, losing a coin-bright ten pounder in the fast drift opposite the schoolhouse on Slick Rock Creek, a tributary of the Salmon River. It was late February, with the feeling of spring in the air. I chose to fish the lower end of the run, thinking that fish heavy with spawn would be apt to lie over gravel. My first cast drifted down, the sinker bumping the bottom at regular intervals. Then it didn't bump.

I hesitated a moment, picturing the river bed as I remembered it, and trying to recall whether or not there was a sudden deepening. Deciding that there wasn't, I struck with my rod tip. A beautiful steelhead arched up into the air, a fish that had been holding the sinker from the bottom by mouthing the bait. I had him on for a short run and two jumps, then he was gone.

145

This experience underscores my contention that one of the most important items in steelhead fishing technique is a knowledge of the river bed, its shallows, deepenings, contours and currents. The steelhead lost on the Slick Rock run might not have been lost had I struck against it a moment sooner. I would have struck sooner if I had a clear mental picture of the stream bottom when my sinker suddenly stopped striking in the drift.

I had known the bottom of this particular run well a year previously, but had not visited it this season. My memory had grown dim, and changes could have occurred. A point that I wish to stress here is that if this fish had taken my bait in its mouth after I had made several casts, I would probably have struck sooner and hooked it deeper. Having made several casts and drifts, I would have had the bottom of the run mapped out in my mind. Mapping the stream bed with a sinker is the technique I mentioned in connection with salmon drift fishing in a previous chapter.

I first became interested in this technique one day on the Rogue River below Gold Ray Dam. This particular stretch of water is closed to steelhead angling now, but twenty years ago when this fishing experience occurred, it was the hottest spot on the Rogue. When I arrived on the riverbank that day, there were several anglers strung out on either side of my chosen casting position. We fished together for an hour and more without taking a single fish. Then another fisherman came down the bank to join us. He strung his gear, baited his hook with roe, and took two steelhead with two casts.

When such an amazing thing occurs, the man who starts mumbling about luck is muffing an opportunity to learn something. I knew that this fisherman knew something that I didn't know, and that I was anxious to learn. I asked him why he'd been able to take two fish so quickly, when he was using the same gear and bait that we were. His reply started me experimenting with stream bed mapping, current power, and trends with a drifting sinker.

"It's really very simple," my chance-met fisherman told me. "There's a ledge out there which breaks off abruptly into deep water. The steelhead are lying right behind the ledge break, where it will protect them from the force of the current. You fellows have been drifting right over the edge of this ledge, and above the heads of the fish, so your bait sinks behind them where they don't see it."

"I see," I said. "But you were casting to the same spot that we were. Why didn't your bait drift over the fish?"

"Well," he said, "I know exactly where that ledge break-off is. When my bait drifts to that point, I suddenly slack off on my line, taking all current drag away from it. This causes my sinker to drop right over the lip of the ledge instead of letting the current sweep it right over."

"How does it happen," I asked, "that you know exactly where this ledge breaks off in such high roily water?"

"That's easy," he told me. "In the first place, I saw it when the water was low and clear in the summer. Even if I hadn't, I could locate it with a few casts by noticing where my sinker suddenly stopped bumping on the rock shelf."

When the Rogue fisherman explained this sinker bump strategy to me, I realized that I was waking up about twenty years late. I recalled that Mauris Addis, a Portland furrier, had tipped me off to this technique twenty years earlier. It didn't register with me then. Presenting such knowledge to me at that time in my steelheading experience was like giving a third-grader a book on advanced mathematics.

Mauris Addis and I had come down to the river that morning at gray dawn. Addis had taken a steelhead and a late-run silver in the first hole above tidewater. We had then moved up to where the roaring current was sweeping beneath the Rose Lodge Bridge. A group of anglers were hard at work, and when we joined them they complained that they had been fishing for hours without a strike. Addis asked permission to try a few casts in the same water. On the first cast he laced into a steelhead. I was then at the stage of steelhead fishing development (a phase we all have to go through before we become steelhead veterans) when I still believed in luck. But I did ask Addis how he had accomplished this feat. His explanation was similar to that of the steelheader on the Rogue.

"There's a ledge out there," he told me, "that breaks off abruptly into very deep water. These fellows have been drifting over the break-off to let their bit sink far below. The fish are right behind the ledge face, protected from the current force."

I could have saved twenty years of effort had I listened more closely. Steelhead tend to travel upstream along certain routes in a river, year after year. They rest in certain areas, and they feed in certain places. Their pattern in a given stream changes only when the stream bed changes and the current threads alter. They do this just as you and I follow the same route to school, perhaps climbing over a fence here, stopping to pick berries there, climbing a tree next. As the steelhead knows the travel, feeding, and resting places in a stream, so should the steelhead fisherman know these same places for best success.

If a fisherman has the time, inclination, and opportunity to study a stream bed when the river is low and clear in summer, these steelhead travel routes will be revealed. One can see ledge breakoffs, which will afford the fish protection from the current, and the shelving up of gravel at the foot of pools an runs, which divert current flow over the heads of fish, allowing drifting food to settle. The gradation of the stream bed's bottom taper from shore to shore will disclose where the deep travel channels are. Large boulders, which are hidden from view when the river is swollen with winter rain, can be seen clearly in summer. Such boulders not only offer steelhead resting spots, but also divert the current to produce back eddies. The angler who knows his stream well will take steelhead.

Approaching a steelhead stream for the first time during high water, or arriving on its banks after a season's absence, what is concealed from the eye can be detected by mapping the bottom with a drifted sinker. A sinker hitting with frequent, heavy thuds is moving over a river bed studded with large stones. Fish do not lie here.

A sinker bumping bottom then suddenly drifting without bumping is drifting over a sudden deepening, where fish are inclined to lie. A sudden slacking off of line will drop the lure into such a pocket.

A sinker moving along with a dragging motion, with uncountable, light bumps, is meeting an upshelving of fine gravel where steelhead not only lie, but also feed. Here bits of floating food tend to settle, and crawdads linger.

When the sinker is moving downstream, but the line tends to curl back at the surface, there is a current back eddy. Steelhead are found here with their snouts downstream instead of up. In such instances the wise fisherman coaxes his lure into the back eddy current. I took the largest steelhead I ever have taken on the Rogue River by coaxing my roe bait into such a back eddy.

149

I had been drifting the Rogue with a guide that day. It was bitterly cold. I had taken one steelhead, and the time was at hand to go home. Because it was so cold, I asked my guide to put me ashore so that I could walk back to where I had parked my car by the Gold Ray Dam. I could warm my blood with exercise. Walking along the shore, I encountered my good friend Frank Worrell of Medford. Frank told me that he had been fishing this particular spot for a couple of hours without a strike. I cast out, noticing that as my lure drifted through the run to settle where his was, it hesitated at a certain point. Then it moved on, but the line bellied back, indicating a back eddy beneath. On the next cast, I coaxed my lure to leave the current flow downstream and enter this backflow. Instantly I hooked into a really big steelhead.

I'll never forget the excitement of that battle. The fish was so big and wild that I knew I'd have to play it carefully, and that I should make no effort to land it until it was thoroughly exhausted. But Frank Worrell had no such ideas. He peeled off his coat, rushed out into the river, and made strenuous attempts to engulf the fish in the garment every time it came to the surface. I was yelling at him to stand clear. He was yelling at me to bring the fish within reach. A good time was had by all. Fortunately there was a bit of sandy beach at hand where I finally managed to land that beautiful steelhead.

On another occasion, my wife missed out on one of the best runs of steelhead I have ever encountered through lack of knowledge of the stream bed conformation. We were fishing with Cliff and Blanche Lemire on Three Rivers, a tributary of the Big Nestucca at Hebo. There were numbers of fish before us. I placed my wife at the best spot in the various runs, expecting her to take her limit in short order.

Passing that way an hour later, I found that she hadn't had a strike. I couldn't understand this, till I realized that she had been casting to the center of the stream, where she supposed the water to be deepest. But in this particular spot, the bottom moved from the far shore at a gentle slope to its deepest point on her side of the stream. The deep steelhead travel channel was within fifteen feet of where she stood. I knew this from having mapped the bottom many times previously with my sinker. I had supposed that she knew this, too. I made a cast to illustrate the point, and hooked a steelhead at once.

From November through March, winter steelhead offer more angling opportunities in Oregon than any other game fish. Summer steelhead rivers, and late spring rivers which are open to steelhead angling, furnish fishing from spring to fall. These rivers are the Columbia and Willamette and some of their tributaries, such as the Clackamas, Molalla, Santiam, Eagle Creek, and the Deschutes. The Rogue and Umpqua have both summer and winter runs.

Summer steelheading opportunities depend a lot on water and weather conditions. If the water is high and roiled, as it may be on the Columbia, one should use winter techniques. A popular method on the Columbia is to cast out a spinning or wobbling lure with a sinker heavy enough to lie where it lands, and let the current do the work. Summer steelheading with flies, a popular method on the Rogue, Deschutes, and Umpqua, is the absolute zenith in steelhead angling. I have done a great deal of this on the Rogue above and below Medford and Grants Pass.

Winter steelheading is, however, the most extensive big game trout fishing of the state. Steelhead streams thread the coastal strip like the veins of a man's hand. Moving south from the Columbia River toward the California border, we encounter the following major winter steelhead rivers along Highway 101:

Nehalem, at Wheeler
Wilson, at Tillamook
Trask, at Tillamook
Kilchis, at Tillamook
Big Nestucca, at Hebo
Little Nestucca, at Cloverdale
Beaver, at Hebo
Salmon, at Otis
Siletz, at Taft
Yaquina, at Newport
Alsea, at Yachats
Siuslaw, at Reedsport
Smith, at Gardner
Coos, North and South, at Coos Bay
Coquille, at Coquille
Sixes, at Sixes
Elk, at Port Orford
Rogue, at Gold Beach
Pistol, at Pistol River
Chetco, at Brookings
Winchuck, at Winchuck

Just how many steelhead are taken from these various coastal streams each year is problematical, for though anglers are supposed to punch their steelhead cards and turn them in to the Department of Fish and

Wildlife so that an accurate count can be made, it is doubtful that all do. Certainly the biggest producers of these big trout, having both summer and winter runs, are the Rogue and the Umpqua, topping the eight-thousand mark.

I would say that the Big Nestucca is the next best producer of the coastal rivers, topping the six-thousand mark, and it is followed closely by the Nehalem, Alsea, Siletz, Siuslaw, and Coquille. The Sixes and Elk are top steelhead rivers, but being farther from large centers of population, they produce only about a thousand fish each year. And these are not all the coastal rivers.

No doubt about it, Oregon's steelhead waters, including both coastal streams and the Columbia with its tributaries, offer the finest big game trouting in the nation for anglers willing to pull on boots, don raincoat, and get out there in the soft rains of winter.

I once lived on the Rogue and have fished the summer and winter runs on both the Rogue and the Umpqua. I would say without hesitation that I much prefer the shorter rivers of the coastal strip for winter steelie angling. The freshest and wildest fish are the steelhead closest to the ocean. On short streams like the Nestucca, Salmon, Wilson, and Trask (to name but four) you angle for fish that have often been out of the ocean only hours, or even minutes. They have sea lice on their tails, are fat and silver bright, and they run quite a bit larger on the average than do the steelhead of the Rogue and Umpqua, or the Klamath.

Although my largest steelhead taken on the Salmon River at Rose Lodge weighed only twenty pounds, quite a number of winter steelhead taken from these short coastal streams have topped twenty-five pounds. That's a lot of trout to lace into in narrow, brush-overhung quarters, in fast water. You have something to tell your grandchildren about when the time comes to lean back in your old-age rocking chair, believe me.

A stranger visiting these streams need have no difficulty locating the best producing pools and runs. Over a period of years these sections have been fished by many and have proved their productiveness. Along the highways, along the forest roads which generally follow these rivers inland from the sea, an observant angler will note where cars have been frequently parked on the shoulders of the roads. Investigation here will usually disclose well beaten paths leading down to good water.

Every angler has his favorite spots. Mine are the Rose Lodge Bridge Hole and the Leaning Tree Hole on the Salmon, the Peg-leg and Farmer Creek holes on the Big Nestucca, the Bridge Bend Hole on the Wilson, the Sand Dune Hole on Ten Mile, the Cedar Creek Hole on Three Rivers, the Big Eddy Hole on the Siletz, the Fallen Tree Hole on Slick Rock, and the Christmas Tree Hole on the Siletz.

Bear in mind that Oregon law permits licensed anglers to go upon stream banks between high and low watermarks, but one must reach the banks over public property or have permission to cross private. Fortunately, few Keep Off signs blossom along these streams. We pray that all fishermen will so conduct themselves that they will continue to be made welcome by landowners.

Here on the coastal rivers in winter, when the multitudes who live in colder climates lay aside their fishing rods to await the coming of spring, Oregon anglers enjoy their best sport. The greatest thrill in fishing is surely when a steelhead strikes the drifting lure, then leaps out of the water in a lash of spray. When a fisherman yells, "Steelhead on," as he fights a whipping rod, he is really living.

STEELHEADING EXPERIENCES

To WRITE OF STEELHEADING, I find I must wander all over the Oregon country and leapfrog across the seasons. This adventurous fish thrusts its snout into all waters of the state which run to the ocean. Steelhead journey up the Columbia and into the Snake, and they are caught in Idaho on the Salmon River.

The steelheader who wishes to make the most of opportunity the year around should start fishing for steelhead in November on the short coastal rivers. The steelhead season closes there on the last day of March. By that time the rivers tributary to the Columbia (such as the Sandy, Clackamas, and Molalla) have fine runs of steelhead in their waters. Eagle Creek, a tributary of the Clackamas, is particularly good during the spring months.

Summer run steelhead are in the Columbia in numbers from June on. The beaches of Sauvie Island below Portland attract hundreds of summer run steelhead anglers each year. These fisherfolk come from all states of the Union and from many foreign countries. One summer I covered the Sauvie Island beaches for an article for *Sports Illustrated*, and found myself mingling with one of the most enthusiastic crowds of steelheaders I have ever encountered.

The Deschutes River, a tributary of the Columbia, is the favorite of many Oregon anglers for summer fish. In August, the famed summer runs are on in the Rogue and the Umpqua.

Some of my most trying steelheading experiences came when I resided on the Rogue River at Medford right after the end of World War II. During the war I had been engaged as a final flight rigger of bombers for Lockheed Aircraft Corporation. When I moved to the Rogue Valley I tried to make up for fishing time lost during the war. Unfortunately the material being manufactured for use as leaders in those days was of dubious quality.

The summer run steelhead of the Rogue demand hair fine tippets in the clear water. It wasn't until after I had lost several steelhead on the jump that I took time to read the fine print on the leader package. It was written that the material should not be used in ice-cold water, since this would cause the leader to become brittle. Now the summer steelhead of the Rogue may average smaller than the winter fish, but they are really wild. Hooking one in fast water on a brittle leader is worse than being up a creek without a paddle. After I had lost a few fish on these leaders, I began to look for a better way.

I purchased some woven wire leaders of great breaking strength. By unraveling these, I obtained a single strand that was quite strong. While Rogue River steelhead were not overly inclined to hit flies fished on this stiff leader material, I did manage to fool a few. And once I hooked into one, I really had him. Since the shores of the Rogue are wide between the winter high watermark and the low water level of summer, I had a running area. Folks passing by on the Crater Lake Highway above Medford saw me rushing up and down the river in a state of wild excitement, and often pulled off on the shoulder to watch the show.

I have a habit of yelling when hooked into a wild fish. This is a way of letting off steam which almost brought me to grief on several occasions. For one thing, my lower dentures fit rather loosely and are apt to fly out at such times! I once caught my lower plate in midair while playing a cavorting steelhead. Nevertheless, I like to fish with a man who yells, or otherwise exhibits exuberance. I know then that my companion is enjoying himself. Deliver me from the fellow who plays a fish wooden-faced, as he might wash dishes. To meet the ultimate in fishing action without smile or cheer seems to me to be out of character. So I yell. One of the most enthusiastic yellers of my acquaintance is Wendell Boyes, Newberg tackle dealer. He is also one of the state's most expert steelheaders.

I once encountered a pair of steelhead fishermen on the Big Nestucca who were making the atmosphere ring with their handling of a big steelhead. I watched them from a nearby rise. One man was hooked to the fish, which he was chasing up and down the bank. The other fellow was chasing his companion waving a gaff. The man with the rod stumbled and fell, and the fellow with the gaff galloped right over his prostrate body. I gathered that they were having a good time, though I'm sorry to report they eventually lost the fish.

During my years of steelhead fishing I have suffered many such defeats. However, defeat in the determined angler brings about eagerness for success. Such eagerness encourages thought, investigation, and eventually knowledge. This is the game where no man ever knows it all, or even most of it. Perfecting the cast and the slow, close-to-the-bottom drift require lifelong study when you're up against the wild torrents of Oregon.

For instance, slacking the line when the lure lands in fast current is a technique of the drift that many steelhead anglers have failed to master, or even recognize as necessary. One day in January when fishing with a group in two boats on a float trip down the Siletz River, while the action was photographed by Don Hobart of Portland for the show *High and Wild*, one of our anglers failed to catch a steelhead all day, though other anglers took them quite easily. He did not slack line as his casts landed. This was proven on two occasions when he handed his rod to others as he paused to light his pipe. On both occasions the other anglers took fish on his rod.

The angler who takes steelhead on a fast river must know enough about water and the lying places of steelhead to select a proper point for his cast. One acquires this knowledge by experience, either by trial and error, or by having an experienced fishing friend share his knowledge of the river. An angler must learn how to handle a rod to get the lure to the right spot, and how to drift the lure slowly close to the bottom at that spot. This is particularly important when drifting a river in a boat, where there is no opportunity to try again.

If you cast into a fast river without slacking line as the cast lands, the current will pull the line taut and cause the sinker and lure to sweep around fast as a whiplash. Consequently, the lure will not sink at the chosen spot, but far below it. By this time the boat will have drifted beyond the selected place, and the opportunity is lost. Again and again I see this occurring on steelhead rivers. To overcome the problem any other way, the angler would have to put on so much sinker weight that the cast would be spoiled by the landing splash, and the set-up would continually snag on the bottom.

Slacking line as the cast lands is accomplished by instantly lowering the rod tip, then lifting it sharply to roll line off the spool. With a conventional reel, lift your thumb from the reel spool as you do this. With a spinning reel, take your extended finger from the spinning reel spool. This is a simple operation, but it must be properly timed and practiced constantly till it becomes a fixed habit. To prove to yourself that this is necessary, cast across swift water with a reasonably light sinker, and give no slack line as the lure lands. Note how quickly current drag develops between rod tip and lure, speeding the drift of the lure and preventing its sinking. Now cast again, instantly giving slack line when the cast lands. Note that the lure sinks at once.

This trick worked on the Alsea for Ted Trueblood and me as we drifted the river with an Alsea River guide. It was February, with the river high and roiled. The guide had beached the boat on a sand spit. He indicated that we should cast to the far shore, close to where the bank was heavily covered with brush that came right down into the water. After we had made several drifts without a strike, the guide grew puzzled.

"This is one of the best drifts on the river," he told us. "I know the fish are there."

I realized then that we were not giving slack line fast enough as our casts landed.

"Slack line fast," I told Ted. "We're drifting too high."

Ted is a man who doesn't need to be tipped off more than once. On our next casts we both got strikes and hooked fish. Playing steelhead simultaneously with Ted Trueblood, whom I consider to be the top fishing authority of the nation, was a real thrill. We hooked sixteen steelhead that day on the Alsea. We released all but three. Some of them were released, as Ted put it, "at thirty yards on the high jump."

The summer steelhead fishing riot that occurs on the Sauvie Island beaches is one for the book. Fisherfolk sometimes line up to fish shoulder to shoulder. With that many lines in the water, one cannot drift-fish, for the lines would become entangled. So anglers put on enough weight to keep the cast where it lands, often using as much as four ounces of lead. Above this they attach lures that will spin in the current. The Oakie Drifter, Cherry Bobber, and fluorescent yarn-decorated spinners are popular. Then fishermen thrust their rods into the sand to await developments.

The real excitement opens here when a fish is hooked. The wild steelie leaping about on a long line gathers in other lines within a hundred yard radius. This gathering in of lines brings jerks to many rods, and fisherfolk leap into action all down the beach. They grasp their rods and begin playing the fish. Each man is certain that it is on his rod, and no amount of yelling back and forth will convince him otherwise. Meanwhile, the fellow who actually has the fish on is lost in the shuffle.

When the steelhead is finally brought to shore by joint effort, it is entangled in a maze of lines and lures. No angler gives up his or her claim to the fish until the lines are untangled to bring proof. When the various claimants discover their error, they are never shame-faced about it. Apparently this is all in the game. Of course, care must be taken that the lure does not fall out of the steelhead's mouth while the lines are being untangled! If this does occur, the steelhead becomes anybody's fish, and it usually falls to the creel of the angler who talks the loudest and most convincingly. That no brawls develop while all this is going on is a feather in the cap of good sportsmanship.

An even more unusual steelhead riot breaks out each summer on the Columbia below Bonneville Dam. From the north shore of the island which thrusts out from below the dam, and which can be reached from the dam itself, steelheaders cast into the fastest and most boulder strewn water in Oregon. Here the air is scented with the mist of Bonneville's falls, while the thunder of falling water stuns the ears. This is very productive steelhead water for those who have mastered the cast well enough to get down near the bottom without continually becoming snagged on the rocky river bed. A big steelhead hooked here (and they run large in this water) usually takes the fisherman down the rock-strewn way at a high gallop. Pursuing a steelhead here is a prime way to gather shin bruises.

Another spot where steelhead excitement rises to feverish heights in spring and early summer is along the banks of Eagle Creek, a tributary of the Clackamas. The fish here have run up the Columbia to the Clackamas, and up this stream into tiny Eagle Creek. Once I saw a fellow here hang his lure in a tree and angrily yank it loose. The stretched monofilament line, reacting like a rubber band on a slingshot, hurled the sinker at the fellow with such force that it struck him between the eyes, downing him as if he'd been poleaxed.

This can be a frustrating stream. Steep banks rise sharply beside the stream, and anglers climb precariously down to the rushing water to engage the fish, which often douse them in the drink, forcing them to wade green, cold water to their shoulders. Still, men, women, and kids pursue steelhead here. I have seen anglers lined up below the deadline marker at the Eagle Creek falls shoulder to shoulder, playing steelhead in a fine froth of leaping excitement. Downstream from this point are several good steelhead pools and runs below the steep cliffs. Fishermen have to climb precariously down to the water's edge, where standing and casting room is conspicuous by its absence.

On one occasion I was fishing there when a fellow laced into a really big steelie. He was unable to control it when it turned downstream with determination. This angler proved to be a staunch fellow who would not admit defeat. He began following the fish downstream, and since I was anxious to photograph the play, I went with him. The only way the fish could be followed was by wading up to boot tops in the powerful roaring current, clinging to crevices in the rock wall, and occasionally grasping a hanging wisp of brush.

At times we braced against the current until it piled up against our bodies, threatening to tear us away from the shore, to sweep us down like fallen leaves. This was one of the few times when I have encountered real danger while steelhead fishing. We spent an hour or more fighting this fish, only to lose it in the end. Pictures I took of this fisherman, braced against white water and fish, keep this experience vivid in memory.

One of the favorite fighting tactics of the steelhead, particularly those hooked in wild winter waters, is the run-at-you gimmick. This is always employed as a baffling fast reversal of direction at the height of the battle. The steelhead will take the line over its shoulder and torpedo downstream, trying to claw its way to the white water below. When it discovers that it can't make it, the fish reverses direction, usually as it lands from a high jump. Then it shoots upstream at full speed, passing the angler, who is usually standing spraddled among the rocks, nerves and muscles still tuned to stopping a downstream dash. When the bewildered fisherman discovers the line hanging loose and limp, he can only reel with all speed, trying to get a taut line so that he will know where the fish is at the moment.

Steelhead have employed this bewildering switch on me so many times that I am always alert to combat it, yet it never fails to reduce me to a fumbling novice. When my hooked steelie shoots downstream, I have all the power on the rod I dare use in my attempt to stop the fish before it goes over the white rapid below. Then,

...grasping an occasional wisp of brush.

when the fish goes into the air, end over end, long as a silver ax handle, I am fully occupied seeing to it that the hook is not snapped loose in the jump. At this precise moment the big sea-run rainbow is usually boring upstream by my position with the speed of a jet fighter. The moments that follow, as I reel like mad to get taut line and resume control, are among the most exciting in my angling life.

We all hope to catch the largest steelhead ever taken, or the largest salmon ever known, but there is one fish in Oregon that grows so large, anglers hope to hook only the smaller specimens. This fish is the great white sturgeon which inhabits various Oregon waters. Below Bonneville Dam the sturgeon is quite often accidentally hooked while one is drifting bait for salmon or steelhead. The fisherman who hooks a large one here in this fast water is into a mix too rugged to handle comfortably. Sturgeon angling, when using a suitable weight of gear, is a top sport in Oregon. This is a fish that handles the man, rather than vice versa. Let's take a look at this sport.

PACIFIC STURGEON

IN ALMOST EVERY FISHERMAN'S LIFE there is one experience that remains more vivid in memory than all others.
To this day, I remember every detail of my midnight
battle with a sturgeon on the Willamette River.

I had set out from shore in a twelve-foot rowboat to
angle for catfish at dusk. Fortunately or unfortunately,
however you may choose to look at it, I used heavy
hooks and leaders which remained in my kit from saltwater angling days in California. The weight of my rod
that night, and the strength of the leader and hook were
sufficient to land a hundred-pound chinook. Yet this
gear was to be little more than an irritation to my
midnight catch.

I started fishing in a back eddy out of the main
current, in what was reported to be one of the deepest

holes in the river, home of some very good catfish. I baited with night crawlers then settled back to enjoy the evening as darkness settled down, a Coleman lantern lit in the bow.

A lone duck beat its quick and urgent way across the sky, silhouetted against the last sunglow in the west. I have always wondered about this lone bird, which almost invariably flashes across the evening sky over any Oregon river. Is it bent upon a rendezvous, or is it an official harbinger of the night? As always, I watched it with a mingling of melancholy and comfort. All was right with the world.

I was brought out of my reverie on this particular night by a tugging on my line. After the proper interval, suitable for a slow-biting catfish, I brought in my first meat for the pan, a foot-long specimen, smooth and yellow. The catfish kept me busy as night wore on. My unanchored boat slowly circled the eddy, requiring only an occasional tug at the oars to keep it out of the main river flow.

I had just glanced at my watch and noted that it was midnight, when suddenly I felt a long pull on my line. I set the hook and came up against solid resistance. At first I thought the hook had missed the catfish and become fouled in a sunken log. I put arch into the rod without being able to move the hook from its position. Sure that I would have to break off, and knowing that my line and leader had at least thirty-five pound breaking strength, I lay the rod down, wrapped line around my hand, and began pulling. There commenced the strangest battle of my fishing life.

I felt the fish move off, then shake itself convulsively and with such power that the hair rose on the back of my neck. I was actually frightened for a moment. I could see the shadow of my legs across the water, magnified to giant dimensions by the lantern light. Suddenly the fish took off. It wasn't the wild lashing run of a salmon or winter steelhead. It was slow, steady, a hard driven home run with such power that the reel handle was jerked from my fingers. The rod arched into a half circle as I started to fight in the only way an angler can when the fish is the stronger opponent. I fought to tire, to wear down, and eventually exhaust.

For the next space of time (it could have been five minutes or thirty) I fought for line. My fish would take out fifty yards against all the power I dared use. Then he would stop and squirm, come back toward me, and run again. When a run stopped, I had no sense of victory, only of vast relief. Finally things began to ease off a bit. I was able to gain line, and I sensed that my opponent was tiring. When the branch of a tree brushed my cheek, I pawed it away and suddenly realized that the boat had been towed out of the eddy. We were now sweeping along in the current of the main river. It occurred to me then that the fish had not been giving line at all! I had merely been cranking my boat towards it, aided by the river's current.

I don't know how long I fought this fish. It was certainly several hours, and it was dawn before I returned to my starting point. At times during the night, I had the fish directly beneath my boat. Then it would move off into the darkness beyond the circle of the lantern's light, drawing my line out to the bare spool. I was only able to stay with this fish because my line and leader were so strong, and the fish fought downstream, giving me the benefit of the current.

Finally, with the fish beneath the boat, I determined to have a look at my quarry. I heaved it to the surface. For a fleeting moment I saw it, and it saw me. It was as long as my boat, and at the sight of me it seemed to make up its mind to quit playing around. Without even a slash of spray, it merely went away, as a locomotive goes away, continuing the run until the line snapped with a report like a pistol shot. I sat wearily in my lantern lit world, while the lap of water against boat, the whisper of the river, the scent of fir forest along the shore seeped back into my consciousness. Such is the power and stamina of the Pacific sturgeon.

In the Oregon country there exists a rugged group of men and women for whom sturgeon fishing is a way of life. They go after this largest of all fresh water fish with powerful rods, strung with lines of hundred-pound breaking strength. They fish the Columbia River, the Willamette below the falls at Oregon City, the Umpqua River, and Siltcoos Lake. Some fish from the shore, and others from boats. They take sturgeon with regularity.

The sturgeon is a fish worth thinking about. This prehistoric monster, with gleaming, opalescent eyes, barbels dangling from its bellows-like mouth, is practically boneless. Its meat is white, firm, and delicious. To take large sturgeon a fisherman must be equipped to overcome the strength of such a fish. If you lace into a sturgeon of any size on salmon and steelhead gear, you're lost. This often happens on the Columbia below Bonneville.

I once saw an angler hook a sturgeon on steelhead gear, and though the fish was no larger than a chinook, it battled with such power that the fisherman had to take off running down the boulder strewn shore. When he could go no further, he decided he'd have to cut his line, but we talked him out of it, and he eventually landed the fish, which weighed only about twenty-five pounds.

Anglers who hook large sturgeon from shore have little chance of landing them. I have often fished from shore below Bonneville Dam, equipped with a husky rod strung with hundred-pound line. The largest sturgeon I have ever been able to land here weighed eighty pounds.

The proper way to fish from shore at this point, where the current is exceptionally swift, is to expect to lose your sinker with every cast, and to rig to meet this situation. Tie a sixteen-ounce sinker off at the end of the line with a cord of lesser breaking strength. Often it is necessary to drive spikes through the sinker so that it will be certain to hang up on the rocks of the river's bottom. If it doesn't hang up, the current will swing the terminal gear around to shore. About a foot above the sinker, tie off a leader not more than two feet long. Use a size 12/0 or larger hook. Bait the hook with a smelt, a section of lamprey eel, or best of all, a chunk of rotten salmon tied on with a winding of thread.

A sixty-pound line and forty pound leader is the most common rig for shore fishing at Bonneville. If these won't hold the fish, neither can you! Now cast out as far as you can. Wait until the sinker hangs up on the bottom in mid-stream, then brace the rod in the rocks, and watch the rod tip. A sturgeon's strike is as gentle as the fluttering of a bird's wing. When you wish to inspect your bait, break off the sinker if it won't come free, and tie on a new one. In areas where the current force is less, lighter sinkers can be employed.

Shore fishing for sturgeon is good sport, but boat fishing offers the best results. Really large sturgeon cannot be handled from shore. Sturgeon taken commercially have weighed in at over a thousand pounds. One taken from the Fraser River of British Columbia weighed eighteen hundred pounds. Several years ago on the Snake River, an angler hooked into a big one that had probably been rooting around in the mire when Paul Revere made his famous ride. A nine-foot long sturgeon may be one hundred years old. They do not spawn until about twenty years old.

This Snake River fisherman had on a real monster. Its weight was never determined, since it finally escaped, but it battled for days, breaking all the gear that was attached to it. At one time in the proceedings, it was racing around the Snake towing a beer keg. And rumor has it that a team of horses was used, pulling a rope that the fish broke. If true, this must have been the grandpappy of all sturgeon.

We write of monsters. However the average angler who desires some sport as well as delicious steaks can have a time fishing for the smaller specimens. It is against Oregon to law to keep a sturgeon less than three feet or more than six feet long. Within this legal range there's good sport and good eating. Of course, you can pit your strength against the big ones then release them unharmed.

I know of an angler who fought a huge sturgeon from his boat below the Willamette Falls at Oregon City. He was forced to cut a ninety-pound line to keep from being pulled into the drink. Another time, three sturgeon fisherman in these same waters had their boat towed beneath the falls by a sturgeon. The boat filled and sank, and the anglers were rescued by a passing tug.

Fishing with two friends here in the 1930's, we took several small fish before hooking a large one. The fish broke my companion's rod, then took rod and reel away from him. The late Ben Hur Lampman, poet laureate of Oregon and long a columnist for the *Oregonian*, landed a sturgeon on Blue Lake that weighed one hundred and twenty pounds. Though the fish had no current there to aid it, the battle lasted two hours and twenty minutes. I saw two five-foot sturgeon taken in January from the outlet of Siltcoos Lake. Much larger fish are hooked here, but usually escape.

The fight Lee Motley and I had with a sturgeon, on the Columbia below Bonneville Dam, was really a honey. Motley is the operator of the Beacon Rock boat landing on the Columbia. Our fish weighed one hundred and eighty pounds and was eight feel long. Fishing from a boat at Bonneville requires considerable seamanship, for this is rugged water. We used a sixteen-foot dory driven by a sixteen-horse outboard motor. Our anchor rope was long enough to reach the bottom in a hundred feet of water, and with plenty of slant, so that the anchor would hold. On the end of the anchor rope we had a twenty-five gallon buoy. We tied the boat to the buoy with a slipknot which could be instantly released. This is standard equipment and practice here. When a big sturgeon is hooked, there is no time to pull up anchor.

We used short, inch thick hickory rods strung with a hundred yards of hundred-pound breaking strength Monel steel line. This steel line was backed with a hundred yards of linen of equal breaking strength. Our reels were Pflueger Pakrons, with wide webbing straps added to the factory drag mechanisms for additional braking power. The hooks were size 12/0, baited with rotten salmon tied on with red thread.

We caught several small sturgeon before I hooked a big one, which appeared to be about six feet long. This fish had the power of the hind leg of an angry mule. It leaped clear of the water, throwing the hook at the top of the jump. A few minutes later Lee hooked his big one.

"Cast off the buoy," he said to me, and we were into the fight.

What impressed me the most about this battle was its silence. Standing in the prow, Motley was engaged with tremendous forces. His knees bent with the strain. Below us the sturgeon fought powerfully, while we whirled in dangerous water. Yet there was no sign of all this violence, no lashing spray, nothing to indicate what was going on beneath the surface except the expressions that flitted across Motley's features. I just sat there, awed by the drama, till Motley's cry brought me back to reality.

"Quick! Start the motor. I'm about out of line."

It seemed impossible that Motley could have lost two hundred yards of line in that silent battle. I started the motor and, since it was apparent the sturgeon was moving upstream, gave the boat's engine full power. I was amazed to see that we were already three miles from where we had started. With the motor wide own, spray curving away from the bow, it seemed an hour before I saw the linen line change to steel on Motley's spool. I kept the motor open until he had regained most of the line, then shut it off. We began drifting downstream again, fighting a weakening fish. When the sturgeon gave up, it gave up completely. It floated beside the boat, eight feet long and utterly spent. We ran a rope through its snout and out a gill, then heaved it aboard.

A quick measurement showed that it was too long to keep, but the Oregon Fish Commission had been asking anglers to bring any large sturgeon caught to the hatchery at Bonneville. The commission wanted a mature male specimen for this pond, where they had a large gravid female, in hopes of being able to raise sturgeon in captivity.

Motley and I had no idea whether our fish was of the required gender, nor, incidentally, did the fish biologists who examined it. But we decided to deliver it to Bonneville, and in as good of condition as possible. We covered the sturgeon with wet canvas and opened the motor wide, heading for Tanner Creek. This creek, which enters the Columbia below the dam, is the entrance to the Bonneville hatchery spillway. When we arrived at the foot of the spillway, we slid the sturgeon into the water and tied it to a post. Then we notified the authorities. Within a matter of minutes a Fish Commission truck appeared on the scene. The fish was weighed, loaded, and delivered to the hatchery pool a short distance away. There it joined a slightly larger female.

I regret to write that whatever good may have come of this was prevented by vandals, who sneaked into the hatchery grounds one night. They drained the sturgeon pool, loaded the two huge fish into some sort of vehicle, and carted them away. The combined value of the two fish, considering both meat and the female's roe, was about three hundred fifty dollars on the wholesale butcher's block, so the thieves got quite a haul anyway you look at it.

When the sturgeon gave up, it gave up completely.

There are many places to fish for sturgeon in the Oregon country. This fish is certainly one of the many jewels in Oregon's angling crown. Another, in my opinion, is the shad. Here we have a fish that has long inhabited Oregon waters, yet whose popularity among anglers has only begun to build in recent years. It's a popularity well deserved. Let's take a look at shad fishing.

SPORTING WITH SHAD

AFTER A LIFETIME OF ANGLING, I would have been outraged if anyone had told me that I would be taken to town by a sardine. Yet this is what happened to me three times in succession the first time I went shad fishing.

Shad actually are members of the sardine family, *Clupeidae*. They weigh in up to a husky eight pounds, though the average runs three to five pounds. Pound for pound, shad is one of the fastest fighting fish in the Oregon country. Given a steelhead's weight, shad would out-fumble the best of us.

A lot of Oregon fishermen are asking themselves how long this shad fishing excitement has been going on without them. Not long, as fishing years are counted. Shad have been in Oregon waters since 1886, when they were planted in the Willamette-Columbia system, but only recently have Oregon fisherfolk pursued them with enthusiasm. I think anglers hesitated because they didn't consider shad a sporting species, nor did they know techniques for taking shad. And in all truth, there is still some disagreement about whether or not shad make for good eating.

I personally think shad are not as tasty as trout or salmon, but some fishermen will give argument to this. It is true that shad have many bones, but these can be softened and made edible by cooking the fish in a pressure cooker, and shad are delicious when smoked. Shad roe is worth a couple dollars a pound on the commercial market, and it is out of this world when rolled in cracker crumbs and fried in deep fat.

Another reason anglers haven't gone after shad is that they didn't know the shad were there. Shad are seldom interested in the bait or artificials we employ with other species. Consequently, a river might be swarming with shad without their presence being detected by fishermen using the general run of lures.

But lately the secret seems to be getting out, and enough fisherfolk are stampeding to the rivers when the shad are in to stir up quite a riot. For some reason this fish seems to bring out the humor and good fellowship in anglers. Jam a group of fishermen close together for salmon, steelhead, or trout, and they are apt to grimly compete with one another. Do the same when the quarry is shad, and a whole different atmosphere prevails, rent with shouts of glee, good-natured kidding, sharing of provisions, and a general whale of a good time. Let me tell you about the first time I fished for shad.

I had launched my boat at Glen Otto's landing on the Sandy at Troutdale. I started out equipped with steelhead gear. I didn't know any more about the fish I was going after than I did about knitting. But I had asked a few questions of those who claimed to have taken shad. Above the Troutdale bridge I started trolling a red and white Pfleuger Pippin, a tiny wobbling lure.

I hadn't gone fifty feet when something slammed into my lure. I thought it was a steelhead as I fought to stop a long hard drive, thumbing down on the reel spool, putting arch in the rod. Suddenly the fish was gone. This happened twice in a matter of minutes. I began to suspect that something was awry, since a man seldom laces into three steelhead in a short period of time. Recalling what I had been told about the shad's tissue paper mouth, I played the next fish real easy and brought him to the net. Even then it was hard for me to believe that a fish this size could have put up such a battle.

You have to play a shad gently, even though it has no intention of playing gently with you. The result is a win-loss record of about one out of three hooked. A shad grabs the lure, hitting it with explosive power, and takes off like its tail's afire. You have to stop the run before you are fresh out of line. And that's only the beginning. This fish fights endlessly. When you finally get it to the point of netting, you'll find the shad is an adroit net dodger. Equipped with reverse gears, it whizzes backward if you try to net it headfirst, and netted tail first, it zips away as though jet propelled. Shad fishing is the only fishing I know of in which an angler hooked to one is apt to take time out to laugh at, and with, a fellow who is trying to net one!

The waters in which shad run each spring in the Oregon country are still uncounted. There are usually shad in the Columbia River system in vast numbers by mid-May, including the Sandy River, a big tributary east of Portland. Shad are also taken at the mouth of Tanner Creek below Bonneville, and in the Willamette below the Oregon City falls. I wouldn't be surprised to find that shad run in all the tributaries of the Columbia and Willamette.

Other shad hot spots are the North and South Coos rivers on the southern Oregon Coast. The Umpqua has a shad sport fishery, as does the Smith. A few shad have been accidentally taken in the Siletz at Taft, and I was reliably informed that shad run up the Alsea in such numbers that they are an annoyance to trout fishermen who happen to be using small wobblers as lures. I suspect there are shad runs in many other coastal rivers as well.

Generally speaking, anglers seeking shad can find them in the rivers from the latter part of April to the latter part of June, with runs starting up the more southerly rivers a bit earlier than further north. I usually plan to be on the Coos River in May to enjoy the shad run. It isn't hard to spot their schools. Shad leap and cavort a great deal when they first come in, though they are often more interested in amorous pursuit than in taking the lure.

With shad, the lure is the important item. They seldom hit plugs, spoons, spinners, or wobblers that attract other species. Shad have small mouths and take only small wobbling lures as a rule. The ideal lure is made from a bit of copper sheet, a half to three quarters inch long, and an eighth to a quarter inch wide. Be sure to keep the copper polished to a bright shine.

The lure should be bent to wobble, not spin. Shad seem to prefer a fairly fast undulating motion. Two lures of identical conformation, fished side by side, will often have contrary results. Place both lures in the current of the stream where their action can be seen, and you may note that one lure wobbles differently than the other. Bend the non-taking lure so that it wobbles like the successful lure, and both will take shad.

A spinner is not a good shad lure, though shad will hit the smaller ones. However, take a spinner blade the size of a man's little fingernail, drill a hole in the lower end to take a hook on a split ring, attach a swivel to the hole in the upper end, and you have a good shad lure that will wobble effectively.

These small wobblers demand a fairly small hook, since a large hook would ruin their action. A number six is about as large as a tiny wobbler can handle. Unfortunately this results in a rather shallow bite in the shad's tissue paper mouth. Couple this fact with the dynamite strikes, way-out-there runs, and end-over-end leaps, and you have an exciting sport!

South coast fishermen near Coos Bay take shad on gaudy flies. Northern shad fishermen seldom use this method because their shad streams are high and roiled from snow runoff when the shad come in. However, I have had some success taking shad on flies high upstream on the Sandy River, where the water is clearer.

Shad flies should be tied on number six long-shanked hooks. One fly used successfully on the Coos River is a yellow streamer wing with a herl body and red bead head. Another good pattern has a silver tinsel body, white hackle, white bucktail wing, and a red head. Pink chenille is often used for the bodies of shad flies, and a section of key chain tied crosswise at the head will give the fly sinking weight as well as the appearance of eyes. Some shad flies have an underwrapping of lead wire to take them down. I find flyfishing for shad more thrilling sport than flyfishing for trout, for the fish run larger and hit faster.

You can take shad from shore using wobblers or flies, but boat casting is best for wobblers. Anchor your boat in a favored place, and tie a sinker to the end of the line, just heavy enough so that it can be walked downstream from the boat by lifting and dropping it in the current flow. The sinker must be heavy enough to stay down on the bottom when the line extends from the boat at a long slant. Above the sinker tie a six to ten-pound leader, using a swivel. Tie your lure to the end of the leader.

There is considerable difference of opinion among shad fishermen concerning length of leader, and just how far above the sinker it should be tied. I recommend three feet for both. Now walk your sinker down below the boat, making certain that it stays on the bottom so that the wobbler works near the stream bed. If there are shad about, action will develop before long.

The growing popularity of shad fishing has caused some of the wildest fishing scenes I've ever witnessed in Oregon. Boats anchor side by side to form what is called a *hog line*. Often there are several hog lines on the river, anchored one below the other, closely grouped. I have always avoided hog line fishing for salmon, because I don't usually like to fish in such close proximity to my fellow man. But the more dense the boats in a shad line, the better I like it. A day spent in a shad hog line when the fish are hitting is an unforgettable experience.

So hard driven are some shad runs that shad hooked in one line-up may entangle boats and hooked shad in other lines. Often anglers in several hog lines become entangled in a maze of zipping fish, yelling fishermen, and rocking boats. Shad wrap themselves around anchor lines. Boaters usually pull up anchor when this occurs, which sets them drifting into other boats. Let me tell you, if this were to happen with any other fish, the likely result would be considerable irritation among the fisherfolk. But for some reason, with shad they just whoop with laughter, roar with glee, and kid each other unmercifully. I take off my hat to this fish of good fellowship.

If you take a close look at a shad you will see why it is such a fighter. Its body is deep and compressed, stream-lined like a jet bomber. The males weigh considerably less than the females. Shad are characterized by a savage initial strike. I have seen them break ten-pound

Shad wobbler

swivel

streamer fly

spinner blade

White
Streamer fly
with red head
& yellow
body

Boats anchor side by side to form what is called a "hog line".

leaders on a strike against a stiff rod and a fisherman who reacted powerfully. An angler who was fishing beside me on a Sandy River shad line broke his ten-pound leader on a strike, toppling over backwards in the process. He looked cautiously around to see if anyone had observed his humiliation. Noting my eyes upon him, he queried plaintively, "What in hell was that?"

Yet another example of shad bewilderment was a gentleman from the East whom I chanced to meet on the upper Sandy. He had a shad on a fly rod and was playing it so skillfully that I felt sure he was a fisherman of vast experience.

Experience began to wear a bit thin, however, when it came to netting the prey. Standing knee deep in water, he unslung his net, holding rod high in the approved fashion. The shad ducked and dodged, then went into reverse and out of reach. It circled the angler like a hound dog around a bear at bay, then wound the line around his boots until he was practically hobbled. In desperation, he popped his knees apart and thrust the net between them, front to rear. With the shad in the net, he then found it temporarily impossible to pull the flopping fish back through his hog-tied legs. Losing his balance, he sat down on the fish, water to his armpits, and with a most disgusted look on his face.

"Man and boy," he declared, making no attempt to get to his feet, "I have fished for trout—rainbow, brook, and brown. Never have I seen anything to beat this flat-sided, paper-mouthed herring. I just don't understand it."

Neither do I. But I do understand that this is exciting fishing. It will be years before we know as much about shad as we do about trout and salmon. At present we don't know how far upstream they spawn, or if they spawn on rocks, gravel, mud, or in the trees for that matter. But there are Oregon rivers to explore for shad, and those with known runs to fish. There are lures yet to be invented, and flies to dress for this quarry. And to the confirmed fisherman, this kind of investigation is as meat and drink.

For those who wish to take shad without wasting time on the search, if indeed time is ever wasted when fishing, I suggest hitting the Columbia River below the mouth of the Sandy, the Sandy itself from its mouth to five miles upstream, Tanner Creek below Bonneville Dam, and the Willamette below the Oregon City Falls from mid-May through June. Hit the North and South Forks of the Coos River by the first of May, and don't overlook the Coquille, the Umpqua at Reedsport, and the Alsea at Waldport. In other streams. This hard-hitting sardine is one of the most enjoyable sports in the Oregon country.

THE PLEASURES OF PANFISH

WHEN LEWIS AND CLARK CROSSED the Rocky Mountains
to explore the Oregon country in 1805, there were no
pond fish here worthy of the name. There were bony
chub, sucker, and squawfish (so named because they
were easily taken by Indian squaws for roasting over
aboriginal campfires).

The settlers who followed the western tide of empire
over the Oregon Trail were at first delighted with the
abundance of red-meat fish—firm-fleshed steelhead and
salmon. But soon they began to long for the white-
fleshed fish of their abandoned home waters. Sturgeon,
with its savory white meat, was rooting around in sixty
to ninety feet of water, considerably beyond the limits of
pioneer fishing tackle and skill.

The pioneers longed for black bass, yellow perch,
crappie, and bluegill. They hungered for the bewhiskered

catfish. And they wanted, above all else, to be able to fish as they had fished at home, with a baited hook and a floating cork bobber. And so, because men willed it, the desired species came to the Oregon country in one way or another over the course of years.

One regrettable introduction was the German carp, which was brought to the Sandy River by Captain John Harlow in May of 1880. Because the carp was considered to be a very fine table fish by the gourmets of Europe, Captain Harlow though it might prove profitable on the Portland and Oregon City markets. He ordered the fish from California, where the species was thriving, and they arrived by way of the steamer Elder. He planted them in a pool at Troutdale on the Sandy River, and they were doing well when a spring freshet raised the Columbia River and flooded out the good captain's carp pond. Thousands of carp fingerlings were released into Oregon waters, where they now befoul many of our streams.

Shad, the hard-fighting fish of the previous chapter, were introduced to Oregon streams in 1886 with a planting of approximately with the planting of 850,000 fingerlings into the Columbia River system.

Catfish came to Oregon by way of the Columbia River system in about the year 1883. The original planting is rumored to have been made in Silver Lake in Washington State. By 1888, catfish were being taken in numbers at Silver Lake, and their journey to the Columbia by way of the Toutle River was inevitable. Today several species of catfish can be found in Oregon waters: *Ictalurus catus*, the white catfish; *Ictalurus melas*, the black bullhead; *Ictalurus natalis*, the yellow bullhead; *Ictalurus nebulosus*, the brown bullhead; *Pylodictus olivaris*, the flathead, found in the Snake River; and in some waters, *Ictalurus punctatus*, the admirable channel catfish.

The arrival of the most prized pond fish of all, the largemouth bass, is confused by claims and counter-claims. As far as can be determined, largemouth were planted in the Willamette and Columbia rivers in 1888, either by E.W. Bingham, or by Gideon Steiner, or both. Since this work is dedicated to fishing the Oregon country today, we will let this dispute rest. Sufficient for our purpose is the fact that this most beloved species of panfish did come to the Oregon country, along with the equally popular yellow perch, bluegill, black and white crappie, warmouth or rock bass, pumpkinseed, and at least four species of catfish.

Nationwide, panfish afford more real fishing pleasure to more people than do the so-called prize fish of the Oregon country, but they are often mistakenly considered to be the territory of barefoot boys and unskilled adults, or only for anglers who wish to spend an afternoon or evening loafing on the water. Without detracting from the fact that these fish can be taken in this manner, and are thus the source of much angling contentment, they can also be taken in more sporting ways.

There is no greater angling skill to be mastered than that required to properly handle the bass plugging rod. And there is no greater angling thrill than that experienced when a largemouth bass smashes a lure on the surface. The panfish of Oregon have been, for many years, sort of lost in the shuffle due to the intense interest in trout, salmon, and steelhead. As time goes by, however, I am sure that panfish will assume an increasingly important position in Oregon's sport fishery, and thus take some of the pressure off the salmonids.

I look back on many years of fishing for black bass beside men who were masters of the short bass rod. Under the tutelage of these experts, on the Yamhill River, I learned what I know of this sport. When I was national fishing editor for *Hunting & Fishing* magazine of Boston, I recall writing an article about bass in the Yamhill River. I suggested that the North Yamhill appeared to be half bass and half water. This stream still produces largemouth bass, though it has had to recover from a bad sewage situation. The banks of the Yamhill are overhung with shrubbery, and the bass in the river demanded that a lure be cast directly to them.

In those days, the angler who could not toss a River Runt or a Pikie Minnow into a teacup nine times out of ten at ten paces was considered to be awkward. I have reason to believe that the art of bass casting with a short rod has fallen off in the Oregon country. If so, certainly it is not for lack of good bass waters.

There are thousands of lagoons, sloughs, and potholes along the reaches of the Willamette and Columbia and their tributaries where largemouth bass of respectable size can be found in numbers. It is a little known fact that largemouth bass can be taken from the the Rogue River. I have taken many largemouth lunkers from the Rogue on plugs cast above Gold Ray Dam, below Medford. Many of the lakes and reservoirs of eastern Oregon contain bass.

The sand dune lakes along the Oregon coast are hot bassing lakes. Siltcoos Lake, with a hundred miles of shoreline, is probably Oregon's top bassing lake. Fishing here one spring with Roy McCurdy, who then operated Roy's Dock on the lake, we landed sixteen largemouth in a short period of time, with the largest topping six pounds. Largemouth over nine pounds have been taken here, which is a respectable weight for bass this far north. Siltcoos Lake is one of the premier panfish lakes in Oregon, having large populations of crappie, bluegill, and yellow perch in addition to black bass. Its catfish attract fanciers from far and wide. All waters holding black bass should also be considered good possibilities for other species of the panfish tribe.

Smallmouth bass have never been found in numbers in the state, but they are present in Tahkenitch Lake below Reedsport on the coast, and in the Willamette River above Salem. Ten Mile Lake, north of Coos Bay, is noted for yellow perch and catfish, as well as for its fine runs of salmon and steelhead. Devil's Lake, in Lincoln County, has had good populations of black crappie, yellow perch, largemouth bass, and channel cats, though it has had problems in the past with carp and weeds. Fern Ridge Reservoir and the Long Tom River just east of Eugene are noted for panfish, as is Horseshoe Lake near Newberg. Owyhee Reservoir, a vast body of water along Oregon's eastern border, is a fabulous bass and panfish lake (one of Ted Trueblood's favorites). And the list goes on.

One of the best ways to go after panfish is to desert the crowded highways and take to the tall tules with a boat and camp outfit. Thirty years ago, my wife and I set out in a twelve-foot motor boat to explore the Willamette and Yamhill rivers.

Our voyage began at the village of Lafayette on the main Yamhill River. There were government locks in operation on the river in those days, and the locks operator put us through just as though our tiny craft was a steamer.

Arriving at the junction of the Yamhill with the Willamette, we started upstream on what we thought would be a cruise of several days. Halfway up the first swift riffle we ran into trouble. Our horse and a half motor could make no headway against the current. Forced to turn back, we made camp on the island at the mouth of the Yamhill, which became our base camp. With camp gear unloaded, the boat lightened, we were able to explore the river upstream for a considerable distance.

My fondest memory of this trip is of lying in my bed on the island sandbar, listening to the bellowing of bullfrogs. The night air seemed to quiver as from the beating of a hundred jungle drums. These frogs, by the way, were also introduced to Oregon from the East. For those who enjoy frog legs, Oregon offers as good frogging as any place I have ever visited, with frogs in some of the sloughs growing as big as cottontail rabbits.

Since this trip, I have explored the Willamette, Yamhill, Columbia, Rogue, Siletz and many other rivers by boat, often sleeping wherever night found me, and enjoying panfish in all its varieties. With more and more people taking to the highways during vacation months, not to mention the campgrounds, boating a river or lake with a camp outfit is a fine way to get away from the crowds.

Don't be fooled by the population living along a river. Between its banks, along its crooked twistings, back in its lagoons, civilization is left behind. The lake you have in mind for such a trip may well have resorts on its shores, but chances are there is many a shoreline, bay, or nook where you can find solitude so deep that it sings like a conch shell in your ears, where fish try to jump into the boat, and indignant deer peer from the coverts.

Panfishing is what you make it. One of its best points is that you can shape it to your mood. If you want to relax, bait your hook, toss it out there, and relax. On the other hand, if it's action you crave, tie a streamer fly on a two-pound tippet strung on the torpedo line of a three-ounce fly rod, and fish for panfish as you would for trout. On this rig, crappie and bluegill become worthy antagonists.

The fact that most people still-fish with bait for these species could lead to the misapprehension that Oregon waters have smaller panfish populations than they actually do. Bass, crappie, bluegill, and at times even yellow perch will take still-fished bait only when they are hungry; they will refuse it when they are not. On many occasions I have proven the truth of this observation.

Fishing the lower Yamhill one day in August, we tied up to a fallen tree to eat lunch. As we worked on our

Along a river's crooked byways, civilization is left behind.

sandwiches, we dunked angleworms in various ways without getting a single strike. After lunch, we rigged up with white streamer flies, taking them down with tiny split shot. We wobbled these flies along to produce a fair imitation of fingerling fry, and took crappie and bluegills almost as fast as we could cast.

One of my favorite lures for crappie is easy to make from a bit of chamois skin. Cut a piece an inch long by a quarter inch wide, tapering it to a point on one end. Impale this on the hook, and fish it with a jerking stop-and-go motion.

Crappie will often take dry flies on the surface at dusk, and bluegills will strike dry flies savagely upon occasion. Small spoons and wobblers fished beneath the surface turn panfishing into a sport than can be faster than trouting.

On light gear, using deft techniques, any fish can turn in a good performance. Once when I was returning from fishing the high lakes of eastern Oregon, I made camp on the banks of the Willamette east of Eugene. That evening I went down to the river to cast dry flies for trout. I didn't take any, but I had one of the fastest evenings of fly casting in my experience. Squawfish were concentrated before me, a fish looked down upon by most anglers as being worthless on a rod. Yet these squawfish came out of the water like rainbow for my drifting feathers. Other anglers, seeing the sport I was having, joined me.

We lay so many squawfish on the beach that an old fellow showed up with a gunnysack to pick them up. A friend of mine, who has long since passed away, used to ask me to bring him any squawfish I took from the Yamhill River. He maintained they were a very good eating fish. I personally have never tasted them, but I do know they can be good on a fly and, as they are considered trash fish, one cannot take too many.

With the numbers of panfish we have in Oregon, no fisherman need go without fishing here. If these are not big enough to suit your fancy, if the strength of your arm craves a bigger challenge, there are other bottom fish lurking in hefty sizes in the surf and saltwater bays of the coastal country.

FISHING THE
SALTWATER BAYS

THE MOST SATISFYING REWARDS of a fishing life are not
the fish taken, but the memories of fishing days and
companions, of quarry won and lost. Strangely enough,
some of the most brilliant jewels in my memory store-
house recall days spent fishing for the less exalted
species of the Oregon country—the tidewater harvest of
flounder, sea perch, porgies, lingcod, rock cod, red snapper, and sea bass.

One day in particular stands out above the rest.
Laurel and I, and Marion Huffman and his wife Vivian
had packed a lunch and driven down the Salmon River
from Otis. We took the dirt road that wanders along the
north shore to the Salmon River tidewater and Road's

End. Along the way we stopped to rent a battered dory from a farmer for fifty cents. The boat was tied to a tree at the water's edge, across a meadow aflame with flowers. Contented cows stared at us and our load of oars, lunch, fishing tackle, and shovel.

We bailed out the boat with a coffee can, then rowed across the narrow channel to the sand flats beyond. The water was no more than fifty yards wide, since we had taken care to arrive when the tide was at full ebb. The flats at ebb tide bear little resemblance to the wide bay that materializes when the tide comes into flood. Sea gulls wheeled overhead, screaming at one another as they competed for the tide's leavings. We paused to listen, hearing the pounding ocean surf just beyond the sand dunes. Sometimes we would see spray jetting over the rise. It was a heady atmosphere for a day's fishing expedition.

We beached the boat on the sand flats of the north shore, got out the shovel and our coffee can, and proceeded to dig sand shrimp. These shrimp are about three inches long and delicate pink. They are excellent bait for tidewater fish and can be dug easily on the flats bared by the ebb tide. Thousands of tiny holes in the sand indicate their hiding places.

With the can full of bait, we shoved the boat off and began looking for the best place to anchor. This is an important step, and largely determines the success of the venture. We looked for the deepest spot we could find. With the tide at full ebb the bottom could be seen almost anywhere, but there were a few places where deep pockets of water still hid the sand. Selecting the largest and deepest looking of these, we anchored on the ocean side of the pocket, so that when the tide started to come in, our lines would drift with the tide, flowing into our selected fishing hole.

We rigged our rods and baited our hooks, then cast out and settled back to await results. The best way to rig for this type of angling is to tie a half-ounce sinker onto the end of the line. A foot above the sinker tie off a three foot leader and a number two hook. Attaching the leader above the sinker makes it possible to feel the slightest nibble on the bait.

By the time we had everything arranged, the tide was starting to come in. We knew that flounder would emerge from the places where they were buried in the sand around us, and that others would move in from the sea with the tide. Our deep pocket would be an ideal place for these prowlers of the flats to seek tide swept tidbits. We added our own offerings to the larder, sand shrimp with concealed hooks. As the water began to deepen, the flounder commenced to bite. We took them in sizes, as Huffman put it, of "bathroom windows." They continued to bite until the tidal flow became strong, which was as expected. We knew they would bite again when the tide slowed at full flood.

As the water about us picked up speed,we waited expectantly for schools of sea perch and porgies to come in. Looking around during this lull in fishing activity, we saw that the scenery around had miraculously altered. The sand flats where we had dug shrimp were gone, replaced by a vast bay. The graceful sea gulls were no longer airborne. They perched moodily here and there on snags and on the remains of a sunken vessel.

Our boat had come alive. It writhed in the strong tidal flow. Great gobs of surf-whipped foam rushed by. With this flotsam came the perch and porgies, striking our bait, fighting well in the current. As the time of full flood approached, the perch and porgies stopped striking, passing inland from our position. This seemed a good time to row ashore and eat lunch. By then our appetites were whetted to keenness by the brisk sea air and good sport, and lunch seemed a banquet.

Afterwards, we launched the boat, finding the tide at full flood. The flounder were biting again, and later the perch and porgies returned on the ebb. I hooked something too large to hold. It shot off when I set the hook, snapping the leader. Huffman latched onto a silver fish that leaped all over the place. When he brought it to net we saw that it was a sixteen inch sea-run cutthroat trout. This fish was not due up river until the first rains of August. When its skin dried in the June sun its back took on the brilliant blue color that has given this species its nickname. Although we had caught hundreds of its kindred before, we had never seen this coloration in all its brilliance.

What a day that was. We enjoyed it then, and we enjoy it even more now looking back. Yet we can repeat the same adventure today, except for the fifty-cent boat. Fifteen years has changed very little in tidewater country. The sea still ebbs and flows, the gulls scream, and the fish are there. All you need are boat, shovel, any sort of tackle, and most important of all—a day, a lunch, and good companions.

Fishing in the saltwater bays along the Oregon coast is a grab-bag affair. When you dunk your bait you may come up with anything. The element of surprise is part of the fun. Lurking in the bays, tidewater sections of the rivers, and off the sandy beaches and rocky headlands— are perch, sea bass, sea trout, red snapper, lingcod and rock cod, grouper, and various species of highly colored kelpfish. These fish, in larger sizes, can be taken at sea by venturing out on charter boats available at many Oregon ports, such as Depoe Bay, Astoria, Coos Bay, Tillamook, Reedsport, Newport, and Winchester Bay.

My wife and I went out on the cruiser *Kingfisher* one August in company with Brick Gardiner, well known Newport fisherman. On this trip we employed red and yellow Japanese feathered jigs while angling in about sixty feet of water a couple of miles off the mouth of the Yaquina River. We used sixteen ounces of lead to take the jigs down.

Pacific Oyster

Pacific Razor Clam

Fishing the saltwater bays is a grab-bag affair.

Wobbling the lures up and down close to the bottom we took lingcod, red snapper, sea bass, grouper, sea trout, rock cod and various kelpfish just about as fast as we could haul them in. On one occasion, as I was hauling up a two pound sea bass, a lingcod of about twenty pounds swallowed my quarry in its enormous maw. I was able to land my fish-on-a-fish with the aid of the *Kingfisher's* gaff swinging mate.

Casting into the sea from shore, a common sport in such states as California and Texas, is seldom practiced by Oregon anglers. Yet in the hundreds of miles of public beach that stretch from Astoria to the California border, there is a world of saltwater fishing available to the shore caster. Unlike most other states, where I have been shooed away from long barren stretches of ocean beach, the beaches of the Oregon country are open to the public. Driving down Highway 101, a motorist can park almost anywhere and stroll along the shore.

Just about any angling equipment will do for bottom fish in the bays, but for rocky headland and surf casting, more specialized gear is required. You'll need a saltwater reel (spinning or bait casting). The rod should be long, powerful, and whippy—capable of casting a four ounce sinker. Hip boots or, better still, waist-high waders are essential for success. And some surf casters carry a strong wading staff to help balance against the current or the chance encounter with a powerful wave.

As for strategy, you should observe the beach you want to fish when the tide is at full ebb. Casting without first mentally mapping the area leads to random fishing once the tide comes in, which results in hang-ups and lost gear. Locate obstructions, such as reefs or weed beds that might entangle your cast at high water. You can also identify the travel and feeding channels of the fish. Some of these channels will run parallel to the beach, others may run at right angles. These channels are merely deeper areas in the beach plain, as seen at low tide.

A rise may create a gully running toward the beach from deep water, a depression that will permit food to settle and offer a route for fish to move toward shore. Two rises may have a ravine in between them. A riptide, or a wash diverted by an outlying reef may furrow a groove in the beach floor parallel to the shore.

Unless casting to a feeding groove closer in, surf casters run out with the receding wave, make a cast, and run back with the incoming wave, giving line from the reel. The lure is thus out as far as possible. Favorite baits include portions of clam, a kelp worm, and sand shrimp. Silver spoon or wobbler can also be effective, particularly for sea perch.

Casting from the rocks or rocky headlands can be exasperating. One must be resigned to frequent hang-ups and subsequent loss of gear. Spoons, plugs, and wobblers are well suited to rock casting, though bait is most popular. Successful casting from the rocks requires a calm sea. When a heavy surf is running, fish that usually feed among the rocks take off for open water, disliking the buffeting they receive. And gear is hard to handle in choppy sea. But when the sea is calm, one can take lingcod in large sizes, red snapper, sea bass, sea trout, perch, kelpfish, and sometimes even salmon.

One way to beat continual snagging of terminal gear on the rocky bottom is to employ a cork float, not one of those plastic floats so popular today, which will break against the first rock it touches. If you can judge the depth of water in front of you with any degree of accuracy, you can set your lure below the float so that it will clear the bottom, yet be close enough to the bottom to attract bottom feeders. One of the best baits for this kind of fishing is herring, either whole or in part. You can buy herring at most docks and sporting goods stores, but if you are around when the herring run into the coastal bays, you can catch an unlimited supply by the method known as *jigging*.

Jigging for herring requires a long leader equipped with from three to a dozen silvered number eight hooks. With a one-ounce sinker on the end of the rig, cast into the bay, or merely jerk the line up and down from a drifting boat. Herring are attracted to the flashing hooks, even though the the hooks are not baited. The key to success is to let the first herring that strikes run free. Other herring will chase this fish, striking at the remaining bare hooks. In this way several herring can be brought in at once. Many Oregon anglers use this method to catch herring during August, September, and October.

When fishing the tidewater bays with herring, I used to anchor my boat solidly in a carefully chosen spot. One day, however, I had rented a dory from the Fisherman's dock at Newport. The anchor furnished was a round chunk of heavy iron. I motored a mile or more up the bay to a likely spot, then cast out anchor. This anchor had a tendency to roll in the tide flow, and I couldn't hold the boat in position. I found myself spending more time hauling in the anchor and motoring back to my selected fishing grounds than I did fishing.

I was working like a Trojan, cursing the anchor, the tidal flow, and the sea wind when it began to dawn on me that I was catching quite a number of fish for the amount of time I had my lure in the water. I decided that perhaps a non-holding anchor was a good thing. I began motoring farther upstream, casting out the anchor and letting it slowly give way, drifting long distances. In this way I covered a lot of water and took more fish than usual.

Often in years past I have had fun introducing visitors from the Central States to tidewater fishing. I recall an occasion when my wife and I invited Chris and Millie Kelsen of Scotts Bluff, Nebraska out for a day on Yaquina Bay. We took flounder, sea perch, sea bass, and lingcod. The highlight of the day, however, was an enormous rock cod which fell to my rod. This was the largest of its species that I had ever taken, weighing around eighteen pounds. It hit when the tide was running in at a fast rate, so that the fish had the benefit of the tidal current in its fight against the power of the rod. I had a terrific tug-of-war with this cod, a green-throated, spiny-finned specimen of formidable appearance in the eyes of my prairie reared guests.

When I finally heaved this monster aboard, it leaped about the boat, turning spiny flip-flops and upsetting lunch, thermos bottles, and tackle kits, not to mention my guests. Millie Kelsen sprang to her feet with a scream of horror, and we had to grapple with her to keep her from toppling into the bay. Shortly after this episode, a heavy run of herring came in, which I began taking with flies as one would trout. My Nebraska visitors decided that they had seen everything. When we served them cod and flounder fillets in my Salmon River cabin that evening, they were so delighted with the entire adventure that they have been visiting the Oregon coast every summer since.

One of my favorite spots for tidewater and bay fishing is the Little Nestucca River where it crosses beneath Highway 101 south of Cloverdale. There is a large mud flat below the highway bridge where clams can be dug. Other favorite places of mine are the Salmon River tidewater below Otis, Siletz Bay at Taft, Netarts Bay out of Tillamook, Coos Bay at Coos Bay and North Bend, and Yaquina Bay below and above the bridge at Newport .

On Yaquina Bay the tide runs swiftly between two jetties that extend out to sea. Those who venture here in boats should be experienced with tidal flow if they plan to go below the Highway 101 bridge over the bay. Above the confining jetties the bay spreads out, lessening the effect of tides and providing safe harbor for the salt–water novice.

A mile above the highway bridge on the north shore, there are extensive clam flats. Large Imperial clams can be found here, as well as small butter clams. When the tide is out, large crabs can be enticed out of their hiding places in depressions beneath masses of green seaweed. Crabbing is especially good here, with crabs running larger than in other bays on the Oregon coast. The Yaquina River tidewater offers some of the best bay fishing in the state.

Another favorite spot of mine is Netarts Bay, six miles southwest of Tillamook. Branch roads lead down to the various beaches. In long ago days, lumber schooners came here from all over the world. They dumped their ballast into the bay, and with it, clam seedlings from scores of ports.

There are thirteen kinds of clams in Netarts Bay, including the delicate butter clam, the prized razor clam, and the blue nose. This bay also supports large oyster beds. Though these are privately owned, oysters can be purchased reasonably from commercial outlets by the gunnysack. These fresh oysters, immediately shucked out and cooked, have a flavor far superior to those purchased at the store in jars or cans. And if you have never gulped down a raw oyster, you ought to try it. Raw oysters produce a remarkable feeling of well-being in the stomach, once you manage to get them settled. I admit to shuddering at the thought once upon a time. But when I selected a small oyster, scooped it from the shell, and let it slide down my gullet, I experienced a new sensation and a delightful gustatory adventure. My first raw oyster, taken at Wilson Beach on Netarts Bay, was not my last.

Over the years I have taken a great many bottom fish along the Oregon coast, as well as crabs, clams, and oysters. But there is one spot on the coast where I have some unfinished business. It is called Boiler Bay. There is a rocky headland on the south shore of Boiler Bay (just below Depoe Bay), where it is sixty feet and more down to waves that surge thunderously, even on calm days.

Casting from this headland with a herring as bait, or with a flashing spoon or plug, you can hook fish endlessly. The problem, though, is bringing the quarry to creel. After playing the fish out, one must crank up the face of the cliff without cutting the line on the sharp rocks as the quarry struggles for freedom. This play requires a strong, heavy rod, long enough to hold the fish out away from the cliff face. I've managed to bring up some of the smaller species here, but I have lost uncounted lingcod in hefty sizes. I plan to work out a set of gear to do a proper job of it next time.

You may well ask why I should go to a great deal of trouble to fish over this cliff when I might take similar fish more easily elsewhere. I can only answer that it is the challenge of the undertaking that makes it interesting. It is the same sort of challenge that leads a fisherman to desert a stream where the trout are easy to take, in favor of one where they are exceptionally shy and wary. It just isn't the fish, or their size, that matter. It's playing the game that makes fishing such an interesting avocation. Fishermen are seldom bored, and a person who is never bored is usually happy.

Before we leave the Oregon coast, there is another fine sporting fish available here that I don't want to neglect. This is the striped bass, a favorite on the Atlantic seaboard, ancestral home of our own stripers. They were planted in San Francisco Bay in 1879, 135 fingerlings transported across the continent. From there they moved north, occasionally reaching the Columbia River. Primarily, however, they have localized around Coos Bay and the Coos, Umpqua, and Smith rivers. With sixty pounders not unknown, these fish deserve their own chapter.

STRIPERS OF
THE COOS COUNTRY

STRIPED BASS CAN BE TAKEN spring, summer, and fall
on the Smith River, on both North and South Forks of
the Coos, and on the Umpqua. When I think of striped
bass, my thoughts always turn to the city of Coos Bay
and its hospitable citizens, who have generously shared
insiders' information with me over the years.

Folks down there have more tricks for clobbering
these large game fish than you can shake a casting rod
at. In early spring they still-fish for stripers in the
sloughs of the bay. In summer they drift bait and troll
hardware for them high up the two forks of the Coos. In
fall they fish the bay itself with spoon, plug, and
streamer flies that imitate bait. Charter boats troll for
stripers, and plunkers cast from shore.

207

One of the best trips I ever had for Coos Bay striped bass was when I joined the members of the Portland Spin Fishing Club for a weekend outing. The Portland club had challenged the Coos Bay spin casters to a contest to determine which group could take the largest fish. I had so much fun on this expedition that I can't even recall who won. I do remember that numbers of bass were taken, some of which topped forty pounds, and that I learned a new striper fishing technique.

We were fishing Isthmus Slough, a long narrow waterway within the city limits of Coos Bay. Dr. Omar Noles, Portland optometrist and then president of the spin club, and Fred Goetz, club secretary, accompanied me in Blanche Naugel's outboard cruiser. Blanche was a vigorous woman of advanced years, a Coos Bay fishing guide of no mean ability. She anchored her cruiser to a log raft, helped us rig our rods properly, and assisted us in every way possible.

My previous experience with stripers had been in San Francisco Bay and the Sacramento River in California. I had never fished for them with live bait. On this spin fishing expedition the bait was live mud cats, a three to six-inch long saltwater catfish common to the area. A sinker was rigged above a three-foot, fifteen-pound leader so that it slid freely along the line. The mud cat was impaled behind its dorsal fin, care being taken not to injure its spine with the steel hook. After the cast, the fisherman held a fairly tight line and waited. As a striper approached, the catfish made frantic efforts to escape. The sliding sinker telegraphed its struggle up to the rod tip.

The bass did not attack the bait at once. It seemed to maneuver around the cat for a time. When it did pick up the bait and move away, the fisherman waited a bit before striking. This gave the striper time to turn the spiny cat in its maw and swallow it head first. Then the angler set the hook, and things began to happen out there in the slough.

The fight of a striped bass is characterized by an initial long, hard-driven home run, which is difficult to control. While stripers do not fight as long and doggedly as do chinook, nor as spectacularly as silver salmon, they keep a fisherman's attention for some minutes.

I didn't fish during the first phase of the striper contest, as I was photographing the event. Eventually, however, I abandoned my cameras to take up a rod. I had purposely left my spinning gear at home. Instead, I used a steelhead drift rod equipped with a standard bass reel which, in company like this, was akin to offering a drink of whiskey to members of the Anti-Saloon League.

As I expected, I was subjected to considerable good natured razzing by the spin club members. After a few casts I managed to hook a striper of good size. As I bore down on the reel spool in my attempts to halt that first stampeding run, I was handed all sorts of weird advice from both banks of the slough. Had I lost that fish I never would have heard the last of it. Fortunately, I was able to bring it within reach of Blanche Naugel's skilled gaff.

A tip here for those who have never gaffed a striped bass. You cannot gaff these hard-scaled specimens in the body, as you might a salmon. The thick scales will deflect the steel, and often cost you a fish. Instead, the gaff must be slipped neatly into a gill, or into the bass's mouth.

As spring advances, striped bass in the bay and sloughs of the Coos River move upstream on their spawning run. For my money, still fishing with either live or dead bait in the bay cannot hold a candle to angling for stripers when they are high up the river. In May a few years later, my wife and I spent ten days investigating this upriver fishery in the company of Al Dubbs and Ira Sturdevant of Coos Bay.

When fishing upriver at this time of year, it is very important to know just where to drift a lure. Though we were at least ten miles from the ocean, the tides still affected the river. It ran back up into the mountains on the flood tide and rushed seaward on the ebb. In certain sections of the Coos, large schools of bass cruise in and out with these changes of tide. If your boat is anchored where this movement takes place, you are almost certain to take fish. If you are not, you are apt to return fishless.

Up here the river is clear and fresh, and at ebb tide the water is low enough in most places to reveal the sandy bottom. This allows one to view the bass as they cruise around. An observant fisherman can locate good fishing areas, but you can't beat having a couple of Coos Bay veterans along to guide you to a hot spot! Once our boat was anchored in one of these favored places, we stayed put, since fish passing the boat upstream on the flood tide would pass by again with the ebb. We had packed a jug of water and a good lunch to help pass the six hours between tidal changes.

The trip upstream that May morning was beautiful and fascinating. As we left the low country the water grew crystal clear. Densely forested mountains edged down to the water. Flowering meadows appeared here and there. The air was sharp and pungent, and and it was wonderful to be alive.

Motoring up the Coos we probably could have taken fish by trolling a plug, spoon, or spinner. We saw others doing this with success. Later I did try this method, getting strikes on a silver and red wobbler which had been successful with salmon. Six to eight-inch plugs in shades of red are the favorite here. But on this first trip, our companions were eager to show us the amazing parade of the stripers.

We moved into the chosen spot and rigged our rods. My wife and I used our steelhead drift rods equipped with bass casting reels and one hundred yards of twelve-pound breaking strength woven nylon. Al Dubbs and Ira Sturdevant used spin rods and reels. Ira had loaded his reel with three hundred yards of six-pound test mono-filament. This light line seemed entirely inadequate for coping with such large and powerful fish. I did not learn until later that Ira was out to break a world's record for striped bass taken with spinning gear and light line.

We all used bloodworms for bait. Bloodworms are three inches long and a quarter inch thick. When impaled on the hook, they ooze a red material that attracts bass. This red stuff soon drains away, making it necessary to frequently renew the bait. The bloodworm is by far the best striped bass attractor, outperforming other conventional baits such as herring, pilchard, shrimp, and clam.

We strung the worms on size 1/0 Eagle Claw hooks, changing our sinkers from time to time as the tide affected the current flow, so that the bait would always be held to the bottom. With all four lines out in the ebbing tide, we awaited developments. It was a pleasant wait, but not a long one. After twenty minutes Ira pointed to the water and shouted.

"Here they come! Just look at 'em!"

Peering down into the river I could see only the sandy bottom at a depth of about six feet, and our anchor rope tugging in the tidal flow. Then they came, first by twos and threes, then by the scores, by the hundreds, their great sleek bodies moving with the thrust of the current. They passed endlessly below us, almost within reach of our hands, some that would probably tip the scales at 50 pounds. For a few moments we forgot that we had baited lines out. Then we were jerked back to reality by Ira's cry.

"Fish on. Clear your lines!"

This was met with some confusion as we scrambled to pull in lines and anchors. Al Dubbs was cranking Ira's motor. By the time he got it started, the striper's charge had taken it around the bend, with more than a hundred yards of line stripped from the reel. Fishing from an adjacent boat, my wife and I pulled anchor and followed the fight to see how it would end. Bill Safer of

Cave Junction was fishing with Sam Todd of Wauna, Oregon nearby. Safer groaned, "With that weight of line he hasn't a chance."

That, I realized, depended on how much line Ira had on the reel, and how deftly he could handle it. We were a long way downstream when Ira finally brought the bass, a twenty pounder, within reach of the net. Its dark horizontal stripes stood out vividly against silver sides.

I must take a moment to point out that fishing for large fish with spider web gear is a challenge that should only be undertaken when one is fishing at a distance from others, as was the case here. I have seen fisherfolk forced to wait out a play for hours as a selfish sportsman sought to bring in a big salmon on light line. Here on the Coos, Ira had miles of water in which to play his fish, with hardly an angler per mile.

During our days on the Coos we took stripers and saw and enjoyed many an exciting play, both on bait and trolled lures. At that time the record for striped bass on spinning gear was held by Gordon Peck, who took a striper of 28 pounds 2 ounces on a six-pound line at Long Branch, New Jersey, as certified by the National Spin Fishing Association on October 17, 1957. Before we parted from Ira Sturdevant on this trip, he had taken a striper weighing 36 pounds 8 ounces on his six pound line, and another weighing above forty pounds.

But for me, one of the greatest thrills of this trip was watching my wife play and land a striper in the thirty pound class on her steelhead drift rod, which has a tip hardly heavier than that of a six ounce fly rod. It was strung with a hundred yards of twelve-point line, new from the factory, with a breaking strength at the time of the action of no more than eight pounds.

The most difficult part of handling these big stripers is stopping that first with-the-tide charge. I feel justified in saying that it is vastly more difficult to play such a fish on a hundred yards of twelve pound line without

...the promise of a stunning show of stripers at every tidal turn.

reel drag equipment, than it is to play the same fish on two to three hundred yards of much lighter line with spin gear. Without detracting from Ira's marvelous feats, I wave a flag for my wife's handling of this sea bass.

The first charge of a striped bass is a hair raising experience when delivered against an anchored boat and a hundred yards of line. The stiff tidal flow on the tail of the aroused fish lends terrific power to the charge. We could well understand the local preference for spinning reels and two to three hundred yards of line. I have never had a salmon get as far away from me on an initial dash for freedom as I experienced with these stripers of the Coos Bay country.

Before Ira and Al took us under their wings, Laurel and I had an eye opening experience on the South Fork of the Coos. We were cruising upriver from our camp at Fuss's Trailer Park at the junction of the two forks of the stream. We were in our twelve foot aluminum boat, driven by a seven and a half horsepower Evinrude. Laurel suddenly pointed down into the water and screamed with amazement. We were completely surrounded by great greenbacked stripers. Not yet aware that these fish migrated in and out with the tides, we did not know that this school was not resident to this particular spot. We anchored right there and went to fishing.

Only later did we learn that we should have started the motor and run about a half mile above the fish, anchoring in their path, since the tide was moving upstream. Furthermore, along these migration routes there seem to be certain points where the bass will strike more frequently than others. Why they do this I don't know, and no one I know seems to know. But veteran anglers are familiar with these spots.

Before fishing these southern rivers for striped bass, you would do well to consult local tackle dealers and the area's veteran anglers. Gather all the information you can about where the fish are at the moment, and what they're hitting. Basically, when approaching these waters early in the spring, work the bays and their sloughs. Later, seek the fish upstream on their spawning runs. In fall, hit the lower areas again, for by then the bass are working their way back toward salt. If you are planning to fish upstream without local guides, do it at low tide when the sandy bottom is visible in many places.

If you intend to fish upriver, plan to stay anchored through the six hour tidal change. And as I stressed earlier, bring along water and a husky lunch. Appetites have a way of growing keen in the salt air. A good lunch, good companions, deep clear water running through forest passes, and the promise of a stunning show of stripers every six hours—no fisherman could ask for more.

MAKING YOURSELF AT HOME

OREGON IS STILL A WIDE OPEN COUNTRY, with extensive regions of wilderness and semi-wilderness in a variety of geographic settings—desert, mountains, plains, and seacoast. But the state has a well-developed system of roads, and many of its highways and secondary roads follow waterways. Traveling anglers will frequently find wide shoulders along these roads, purposely constructed to allow anglers to pull off, park, and fish nearby rivers or lakes.

In the settlements and along the highways there are ample and reasonable accommodations for travelers. The greatest concentrations of facilities for fishing visitors are within the valleys of the Willamette and Rogue rivers, along the Columbia River, in Central Oregon near the community of Bend, and on the Oregon coast.

217

For those who prefer to avoid commercial services, Oregon offers an amazing selection of camping opportunities. There are a great number of state parks, many with full service campgrounds for tents and trailers. Established camps on Bureau of Land Management and U.S. Forest Service land number in the hundreds, with many more primitive camps scattered throughout the state's fourteen national forests and extensive range lands. Furthermore, a great many Oregonians avoid camps all together, preferring to pitch their tents or throw down their sleeping bags wherever the night, or inclination, finds them.

Camping out is a way of life in the Oregon country. I venture to say that more Oregon citizens camp out than do those of any other state in the Union. There are several reasons for this. One of the main reasons, as far as I am concerned, is that Oregon lacks what so many other states have in quantity—poisonous critters. There are no copperheads or water moccasins anywhere in Oregon; no tarantulas, centipedes, or scorpions; and best of all, there are no chiggers.

Annoying flies are few in number, with mosquitos bothersome only in limited areas and for a short season in midsummer. During every month of the year mosquito-free camping can be enjoyed by exercising a bit of judgment in the selection of campgrounds. I have only been bothered by mosquitoes in a few camps I have made in the high lake basins in early summer, and along the slow moving waters of eastern Oregon during the months of July and August.

The availability of drinkable water and plentiful campfire fuel, the mild weather, and the indescribable beauty of Oregon's varied landscape make this country a natural for the outdoor camper. In fact, I feel camp gear is essential to taking advantage of Oregon's fishing opportunities, especially those fabulous back country lakes.

Comfortable camping is an art. Writing about camping techniques, I have often been accused of being a softy by those who like to think they are tough, rough, and rugged. I have camped in nearly every state in the Union west of the Mississippi. I have camped in the Rockies, Cascades, and Sierra Nevadas, on the Mojave Desert, and amongst the chiggers and poisonous snakes of Texas from the Gulf to the Panhandle. I have slept on snow covered ground long before I acquired a sleeping bag, and awakened at dawn in a hundred camps to see hoarfrost on my blankets. Because of this, I do not have to suffer today to prove to myself that I can do it. I maintain that camping out is supposed to be a pleasurable experience, not a foray against the Sioux.

Because I have camped out with nothing more than a blanket and a prayer, way back when men were supposed to be as rugged as timber wolves, I might join some of the old timers who express contempt for modern camping gear. But I choose to write about camping as it is possible today, when most of us travel by way of automobiles.

We can take along suitable camping gear to make the experience enjoyable, particularly if women and children are to be included in the expedition. The man who wants to make a camping pal of his wife, rather than send her screaming for Reno, should bear in mind that camping is not supposed to be a test of endurance. I believe life is intended to be as pleasant as we can make it.

Camping out requires exactly the same basic essentials as those needed at home: protection from the elements, a good bed, food cleanly prepared, light, and heat. Your goal is to achieve these objectives in camp without breaking down the springs of the car when on the road, or your back when afoot. This does not mean that you bring along the kitchen sink. It means careful selection of gear for the type of camping you expect to do.

But if something of considerable bulk will make camp more comfortable, I say bring it along when you're traveling by car.

No amount of camping equipment will make up for camping know-how, however. I candidly admit that I have made as many camping errors as anyone. I look back with a chuckle on some of the gear I have used down through the years. When I was a kid on the wind-blown prairie of eastern Montana, I employed a thick quilt which had a unit of warmth to the pound. With this I snuggled up to the cold sagebrush. I later worked my way through a weird assortment of gear which included a folding bed with more cussedness built into it than a hammer-headed mustang. It slept as cold as a lizard on ice.

My wife and I spent our wedding night encamped on the Klamath River in northern California over thirty years ago. We used a double sleeping bag which was so narrow that wind whistled down our backs. Since I had inadvertently placed the sleeping bag in an army ant path, we had more than cold breezes down our spines that night. The fact that my wife is still with me, and camping out with me, is a credit to her staying powers.

In contrast to the above horror stories, I took a trip around the Olympic Peninsula a few years ago to gather material for an article for *Outdoor Life*. Traveling alone I covered over a thousand miles of highway and logging roads, sleeping where night found me. I carried a down filled sleeping bag, a grub box, camp ax and knife, a single burner gasoline stove, a flashlight, nested cooking utensils, and a 7 x 16 light canvas tarpaulin.

With this equipment I made camp in a few minutes and never had more comfortable camps in my life. This was the only trip I ever took where I had breakfast in bed every morning. I merely turned over at dawn to light the single burner stove. I put the coffeepot on to perk, then set it aside after dropping two whole eggs right into the coffee to soft steam to a perfection that suits my taste. While the eggs steamed, I made a couple pieces of whole wheat toast on the stove burner. After breakfast in bed, I was up and ready to roll in a matter of minutes.

I struck no foul weather on this trip, but if I had I could have handled it nicely. The light tarpaulin which went under and over my sleeping bag in good weather would have formed a tent when thrown over a limb and staked down at the sides by ropes through its brass eyelets. With a few fir boughs piled at one end of the tent thus formed, and a fire built at the other, I could have outlasted a snowstorm or a rain.

Proper gear and camping technique are dependent on the length of time one expects to be out, the number of people in the party, and the weather one can reasonably expect to encounter. Tents come in all sizes and shapes. I own three, but I would rather find myself afield without a tent than without one or more tarpaulins. The two most basic camping items in my gear are my down insulated sleeping bag and my light 7 x 16 tarpaulin, which is large enough to go over and under my sleeping robe, with two feet extending beyond the pillow. A tarp should have brass eyelets set every three feet around the edges, with lengths of one-quarter inch rope tied on at intervals. A tarp will form almost any shape of tent desired, and it can be rigged in almost any terrain.

Until you start using a trailer house, there is no substitute for the wall tent, which will permit the use of a wood burning stove with a chimney. Such tents are ideal for stays of considerable duration, particularly when several people are involved. However wall tents are too bulky and awkward for the average overnight or weekend trip. We have found that a standard pyramid tent is suitable for comfortable camps in any but severe weather.

We arrange our pyramid tent so that we have far more comfort in camp than one might expect from such a flimsy rig. We put down sleeping bags on either side of the center pole. If the weather is mild, air mattresses are suitable beneath the bags. If the weather is cold, we take along a couple of large game bags which are used for hanging deer and which are available at most sporting goods stores. These bags make excellent mattresses when filled with ferns, fir tips, grass, or whatever suitable material is available. This forms mattresses that are thick and soft to keep out ground cold and bring the camper to dawn in complete comfort.

We have found that rising at dawn is the moment apt to bring the most discomfort, particularly when frost hangs heavy on the pines of eastern Oregon in late fall. A few carefully selected items will take the curse off a dawn tent rising. We place an eighteen-inch by two-foot piece of Masonite between the heads of our sleeping bags. On this we put a single burner Coleman stove, a flashlight, two pair of bedroom slippers, and a box of stick matches. On the center pole of the tent (and this is why we like the center pole style) we hang a Coleman lantern.

When I awaken in the morning I simply turn over in my warm sleeping bag to light the stove. Within a matter of moments the tiny blue flame takes the chill from the tent. I now put on my slippers, and if it is still dark, I use the flashlight while I light the lantern. This furnishes additional heat as I dress. When I step out of the tent, fully dressed, I have not experienced a moment of discomfort, even on really frosty mornings.

What greets me outside the tent depends on how I used my tarpaulins. In forested Oregon country, we usually can place our tent so that conveniently situated trees will allow us to hang the tarp to shield the area in front of the tent from rain, sun, or wind. If there are no trees available (and I've seldom had such a camp spot in Oregon) the car can be positioned so that tarps can be attached to it and staked down by ropes to shield the cooking and eating area. The greatest drawback to a pyramid tent, with its slanting front fly, is that it does not meet rainy conditions well. A tarpaulin can be rigged to counter this weakness.

Since this type of tent is too small for cooking and eating except in emergencies, a kitchen should be arranged outside. For car travel, many light and ingenious table and chair sets are available on the market. However, pieces of three-eighths plywood, with holes bored in the corners to take stakes driven into the ground, will form tables and chairs as efficient as any you can buy. The holes should be an inch in diameter, and the stakes can be cut before leaving home, or cut in the field.

For this and many other purposes, all campers should carry a three quarter ax with a leather blade shield. We bind our ax together with a small camp shovel, using thick rubber bands cut from inner tubes. Tarpaulins, plywood, tent, ax, and shovel then lie flat in the rear deck of the car and take up very little of the available storage room.

We like to build a campfire, and we like to cook over a campfire when we have time. Aluminum foil is very handy for campfire cooking. Fish, corn, and potatoes bake wonderfully when rolled in aluminum foil and buried in the coals. When we are in a hurry to hit the stream or lake, we use a two burner gas stove with a set of nested cooking pots. And one thing I never fail to do in any camp, particularly when my wife is with me, is to hang a mirror on a tree, with a washbasin and a pail of water beside it.

All this equipment may mark me as a camping softy. But it packs easily in a car, and we do intend to enjoy camping, not just endure it. My liking for tarpaulins stems from the use of the cowboy tarp as a youngster in

Montana on my father's ranch. The Montana days of bedroll and cowboy tarp are now in the past. I suppose we will soon see the vanishing of the tent and tenting gear as well, as today's outdoorsman turns more and more to vacation house trailer and camp coach mounted on a husky pickup truck.

In forest campgrounds today where fisherfolk gather by lake and stream, you will see more vacation trailers and coaches than you will tenting gear. I use a trailer myself. But I always carry along the items necessary to make trailerless and tentless expeditions. In this way I am able to park my trailer in a forest camp and, with sleeping bag and tarp, take side trips to waters where a trailer cannot go. I have not lost my liking for, and ability to undertake, lone wolf trips into isolated fishing waters.

We could fish the streams and lakes of Oregon for a lifetime without having to abandon our cars and trailers, for the value of Oregon timber has made road building essential for fire protection. In many cases these fire roads appear to have been formed by a single pass with a bulldozer blade, but they nevertheless permit the passage of the average family car, particularly in the high and dry eastern Oregon plain where so many of our outstanding fishing lakes are located. I have covered thousands of miles of these forest traces in the deep silence of the Oregon wilds without damage to car or trailer. But the adventurous angler who wants to back away from roads and fish pristine water must still depend on shank's mare and a light camping outfit. Today's freeze-dried food and lightweight gear make hike-in fishing trips more pleasurable than ever before.

Let me say a few words here about safety in the back country. Always let a dependable person know where you intend to go and when you intend to get back. Carry matches or a cigarette lighter in a waterproof bag.

Always carry a compass and, if possible, a detailed map of the area to be penetrated.

A compass is of little use to a hiker unless it is consulted on the way into back country. Always take bearings on distant objects when traveling off a well-marked trail. Note changes of direction. If you use your compass to tell you in which direction you have walked, your watch to tell you how long you have walked in a given direction, and your eyes to study the lay of the land, you will have little difficulty returning. And always believe the compass. Never doubt it. But be sure it is not deviated by being held too close to metal objects. I once came out of the Tillamook Burn in a heavy fog when every nerve of my body told me that I was going in the wrong direction. But I forced myself to believe the compass and came right into camp.

Safety in the woods, or in any wild area, depends more on what lies between the hiker's ears than what is in his pack. Never, but never, permit panic to destroy your judgment. I have never known a hiker to suffer severe penalties from being lost other than those which were at least partially brought on by unreasoning panic. You may never become lost, but equip yourself for the eventuality by being mentally prepared to deal with the situation. These days there is no need for panic should you become seriously lost. You need only build a smoky fire and stay put. Fire lookouts will soon send help rushing to the scene.

Actually, a night or so without equipment need not cause hardship. I was once dropped off by a friend on an isolated stream. The friend was supposed to pick me up before dark, but when his Jeep broke down he was unable to return on schedule. With night closing in and a wind and rain storm developing, I sat down to add up my assets. I had a creel containing some trout, a cigarette lighter, and a belt knife.

Within a matter of minutes I was equipped to spend a comfortable night. Avoiding towering snags left by the fire that caused the Tillamook Burn (and which might topple in the coming windstorm), I went to work. I selected two fir trees about ten feet high. A long fallen limb, when thrust into the heavy boughs of the firs some five feet from the ground formed a ridge pole against which I leaned other branches to form the walls of a four-sided enclosure, leaving a crawl-in opening on the side away from the wind. A covering of fern braken made a deep soft mattress inside the enclosure. I cleaned the duff from the ground in front of the opening to make a safe base for my fire. When the fire had died down to coals, it was an easy matter to clean my fish at the creek and cook them to a turn on green willow twigs. All I lacked was salt.

Mother Nature is apt to cuff the camper who does not obey her rules, even as the mother bear cuffs her cubs when they step out of line. The camper who pitches a tent beneath weak snags, fails to ditch it to keep out rain in heavy rainstorms, builds a fire where smoke will blow into his face, or wears shoes that cause blisters, makes errors in judgment that might be serious—but that usually only result in something to chuckle about in years to come.

Nobody could possibly have made more such errors than I have over the years, yet I have never suffered serious injury when camping or fishing, never been bitten by poisonous snakes or attacked by wild animals. The possibility of injury in the backwoods today is far less than driving to work in traffic.

HOW TO ENJOY
THE OREGON COUNTRY

SOME FISHERFOLK GET MORE out of the outdoors than others—more enjoyment, more sense of peace and good health. These are people who, either by birthright or practice, have learned how to open up their minds and let nature in.

Places of great beauty and solitude like the mountains, lakes, and streams of the Oregon country have much comfort to offer the jangled nerves of modern day men and women, if they can only learn how to let it in to do its healing work.

People keep nature out when they drag along to the field the very things they sought to escape (whether they were conscious of that aim or not). Some of the things people cart along with them are actual, and some are merely mental. I can tell within a matter of minutes after I meet a fellow human being streamside if they are able to enjoy nature to the fullest. I can tell by the way they act.

Some folks I meet at camp have come to admire the sunsets and sunrises, to thrill sleepily to the rise of fish feeding at night. They have come to listen to the river, to the whisper of the breeze in the pines, and to the silence itself. Others, in contrast, do not listen. To me there seems to be a distinct cleavage between the two sets of people. One group comes to the outdoors to get away from home. The other group comes to keep company with nature. More power to both, but I do feel that the first group is missing something of great value.

Few people are able to sit in silent communion with nature. They twist and squirm while their minds chew on all sorts of matters. Opening up to nature silences the inner turmoil and dissolves tension. Eventually, nature's healing power becomes something real enough to lean on.

I have a friend with whom I frequently fish. One evening we were driving down the North Santiam highway toward Marion Forks at dusk. The highway was a straight ribbon ruled by twin columns of tall fir trees, and beyond it towered a snowcapped peak. The motor ran soundlessly. The whole world seemed hushed as if awaiting the fall of night. The evening had me in its grip. I was entranced. My companion leaned over and turned on the radio full blast. He thought nothing of this, yet it shocked me as if he had suddenly begun to curse in a church.

I have never had trouble letting nature in, not because I am wiser than most, but perhaps because as a youth I could not keep her out. As a boy on our homestead in Montana, before we could afford to fence the place, it was my job to mind the cattle on the open range. Unfortunately, my father couldn't spare a horse from harness to accompany me on the job, so at nine years old I was the only cowboy I knew on foot. I walked the cattle out in the morning, stayed with them all day, and didn't bring them home until night.

There was nothing for me to do during the long days, weeks, and months but look and listen. This was a sort of enforced communing with nature that I resented at the time, but have been thankful for ever since. I became accustomed to letting nature knock on the door of my subconscious.

Subconscious is the word, and the key to the whole process. For it is only by taking the conscious mind out of gear and letting the subconscious mind take over that you are able to be one with nature. My premise is easily proven. Go out on your own somewhere where there are no sounds of civilization to distract you. Sit silent and motionless, and force your mind into complete blankness. It will try to trick you, but be severe with it.

As time goes by you will begin to sense everything going on around you in a way you have never sensed before. You may become aware of the whisper of the forest, a thrush balanced delicately on a bush, the murmur of the river, or the way the air blues up in the distance. After a time you will mentally shake yourself awake, feeling as though you've enjoyed a restful sleep. But you were not asleep. You were probably more alert than you have ever been before. Had a deer flapped an ear in the covert, or a mouse rustled a leaf, you would have known it.

If this exercise works for you, it is but the first lesson. Try it again. If you persist, you may discover that nature will enter your spirit not only when you sit quietly and force conscious thoughts and worries from your mind, but also during your active moments. Nature will reach out to you as you fish.

You won't necessarily be thinking about the sights, sounds, and scents of the world around you as you concentrate on the float of a bobber, your tumbling lure, or the drift of a fly in the current. But you will be keenly aware of nature as a partner in your fishing pleasure. And when you return to the daily grind, you will find yourself sharing with others not only tales of the big fish you caught, but also your recollections of the sweet scent of the forest, the song of the river, the call of a loon at night. This is nature's prescription for stomach ulcers and frazzled nerves.

And of all the information that I have endeavored to share with you in this volume, it is the most important tip of all for fishing and enjoying the magnificent Oregon country.